Infinix Note 40 Pro/40 Pro+ User Guide

A step by step tutorial on how to get the most out of your phone

By

Alaina Cox

Copyright © 2024 Alaina Cox

All rights reserved. No part of this book may be reproduced or transmitted in any form or by any means, electronic or mechanical, including photocopying, recording or by any information storage and retrieval system, without permission in writing from the author.

This book is a work of nonfiction. The views expressed are solely those of the author and do not necessarily the views of the publisher, and the publisher hereby disclaim any responsibility for them.

Table of contents

Introduction — 6
Part 1: Getting Started — 8
Chapter 1: Unboxing and Setting Up Your Phone — 8
   1.1 Introducing the Infinix Note 40 Pro/Pro+ — 8
   1.2 Package Contents — 11
   1.3 Inserting the SIM Card and microSD Card — 12
   1.4 Connecting to Wi-Fi — 14
   1.5 Creating a User Account — 15
   1.6 Transferring Data from Your Old Phone — 17
Chapter 2: Getting to Know Your Phone — 22
   2.1 Physical Layout — 22
      2.1.1 Buttons and Ports — 24
      2.1.2 Camera Layout — 26
      2.1.3 Fingerprint Sensor — 27
   2.2 Home Screen and App Drawer — 29
      2.2.1 Navigating the Home Screen — 29
      2.2.2 Adding, Removing, and Organizing Apps — 32
      2.2.3 Accessing the App Drawer — 34
   2.3 Notifications Panel — 35
      2.3.1 Accessing Notifications — 35
      2.3.2 Clearing Notifications — 38
      2.3.3 Customizing Notification Settings — 39
      2.4 Quick Settings Panel — 41
Part 2: Essential Features — 44
Chapter 3: Making and Receiving Calls — 44
   3.1 Using the Dial Pad — 44
   3.2 Making Calls — 46
   3.3 Receiving Calls — 49
   3.4 Call History — 51
   3.5 Voicemail and Call Forwarding — 53

Chapter 4: Text Messaging (SMS/MMS) — 56
    4.1 Sending and Receiving Text Messages — 56
    4.2 Adding Attachments (Photos, Videos) — 59
    4.3 Managing Conversations — 61
    4.4 Blocking Numbers — 63

Chapter 5: Managing Contacts — 66
    5.1 Adding and Editing Contacts — 66
    5.2 Creating Groups — 68
    5.3 Searching for Contacts — 70
    5.4 Syncing Contacts — 72

Part 3: Unleashing Your Camera — 74

Chapter 6: Capturing Photos and Videos — 74
    6.1 Taking Photos in Auto Mode — 74
    6.2 Using Different Camera Modes (Portrait, Macro, etc.) — 76
    6.3 Recording Videos — 78
    6.4 Using Flash, Zoom, and HDR — 81

Chapter 7: Exploring Advanced Camera Features — 84
    7.1 Pro Mode for Manual Controls — 84
    7.2 Using the Macro Lens (if applicable) — 86
    7.3 Slow-Motion Recording — 88
    7.4 AI photography Made Easy: Enhance Your Photos with Intelligence — 90

Chapter 8: Camera Settings and Customization — 94
    8.1 Adjusting Photo and Video Resolution — 94
    8.2 Customizing Image Quality — 97
    8.3 White Balance and Exposure Controls — 99

Part 4: Maximizing Functionality — 102

Chapter 9: Fingerprint Unlock and Facial Recognition — 102

Chapter 10: Connecting to Wi-Fi and Sharing Your Connection — 106
    10.1 Connecting to Wi-Fi Networks — 106
    10.2 Creating a Mobile Hotspot — 108

Chapter 11: Pairing with Bluetooth Devices — 112

11.1 Connecting to Bluetooth Headphones or Speakers	112
11.2 Transferring Files via Bluetooth	114
Chapter 12: Optimizing Battery Life	**118**
12.1 Understanding Battery Usage	118
12.2 Enabling Battery-Saving Features	121
12.3 Charging Your Phone	124
Part 5: XOS Customization	**126**
Chapter 13: Personalizing Your XOS Experience	**126**
13.1 Changing Themes and Wallpapers	128
13.2 Customizing Ringtones and Notifications	130
13.3 Adjusting Launcher Settings	132
Chapter 14: Exploring Unique XOS Features	**134**
14.1 Using the Folax Voice Assistant	136
14.2 Enabling Lightning Multi-Window	138
14.3 Creating Custom Gestures	140
Glossary of Phone Lingo	**142**
Conclusion	**146**
Unveiling the Specs: A Deep Dive into the Infinix Note 40 Pro/Pro+ Technical Stuff	**148**
Taming the Troubles: Troubleshooting Guide for Common Issues	**152**
Frequently Asked Questions (FAQ)	**156**

Introduction

Welcome to the ultimate user guide for the Infinix Note 40 Pro and Pro+, the latest additions to the Infinix family of smartphones. These devices are packed with innovative features and cutting-edge technology, designed to provide an unparalleled user experience.

In this guide, we will take a comprehensive look at the Infinix Note 40 Pro and Pro+, covering everything from their sleek design and powerful performance to their advanced camera system and long-lasting battery life. Whether you're a seasoned smartphone user or new to the world of mobile technology, this guide is designed to help you get the most out of your new device.

We will explore the various features and functions of the Infinix Note 40 Pro and Pro+, including the intuitive user interface, seamless connectivity options, and a wide range of customization features. We will also provide tips and tricks for using the device's advanced features, such as the AI-powered camera system, which allows you to capture stunning photos and videos with ease.

In addition, we will discuss the device's security features, such as the fingerprint scanner and facial recognition, which provide an extra layer of protection for your personal data. We will also cover the various tools and resources available to help you manage your device's battery life, storage, and performance.

With its powerful processor, high-resolution display, and advanced camera system, the Infinix Note 40 Pro and Pro+ are truly remarkable devices that are sure to impress. We hope that this guide will serve as a valuable resource as you explore all that these devices have to offer. So, let's get started and unlock the full potential of your Infinix Note 40 Pro or Pro+!

Part 1: Getting Started

Chapter 1: Unboxing and Setting Up Your Phone

1.1 Introducing the Infinix Note 40 Pro/Pro+

Get ready to dive deep into the feature set of your brand new Infinix Note 40 Pro/Pro+. This section will be your guide to unlocking its full potential, from the immersive display to the powerful processor and versatile camera system.

A Feast for Your Eyes: The Display

Immerse Yourself: Prepare to be captivated by the phone's expansive, high-resolution display. We're talking about a generous size (likely around 6.78 inches) perfect for watching videos, gaming, and browsing the web. The display technology (AMOLED for Pro+, IPS for Pro) delivers rich colors, deep blacks, and exceptional viewing angles. Plus, the Full HD+ resolution (2436 x 1080 pixels) ensures sharp details and crisp text.

Smooth Sailing: Whether you're scrolling through social media or playing fast-paced games, the display's high refresh rate (likely 120Hz) guarantees a smooth and fluid experience. This means less stuttering and a more responsive feel, making everything a joy to use.

Performance Powerhouse: Processor and RAM

Unleash the Speed: Get ready for a phone that can handle anything you throw at it. The Infinix Note 40 Pro/Pro+ boasts a powerful MediaTek Dimensity 7020 processor, built for efficiency and performance. This processor tackles everyday tasks, multitasking between apps, and even demanding games with ease.

Multitasking Made Easy: With ample RAM (likely 8GB or 12GB), you can switch between apps seamlessly without experiencing lag. This ensures a smooth and efficient workflow, allowing you to keep multiple apps running simultaneously without compromising performance.

Storage Options: Store all your photos, videos, games, and apps with the phone's ample built-in storage (likely 256GB). If you need even more space, some models might offer expandable storage via a microSD card (check your specific model for confirmation).

Capture Stunning Moments: The AI-Powered Camera System

Elevate Your Photography: Unleash your inner photographer with the impressive camera system on the Infinix Note 40 Pro/Pro+. The main attraction is the high-resolution sensor (likely 108MP on the Pro+, 48MP on the Pro) that captures stunning detail in your photos. Additionally, Optical Image Stabilization (OIS) on the Pro+ helps reduce camera shake for sharper photos, especially in low-light conditions.

Versatility at Your Fingertips: The phone doesn't stop at just one camera. Depending on the model, you might have additional lenses like an ultrawide lens for capturing expansive landscapes or a macro lens for getting incredibly close to tiny objects. There might also be a depth sensor that helps create beautiful bokeh effects with blurred backgrounds in portrait mode.

Smarter Photos with AI: The phone's AI capabilities elevate your photography game. Scene detection automatically adjusts settings for different scenarios, like switching to night mode in low-light environments or landscape mode for capturing expansive vistas. Object recognition optimizes capture for specific subjects, ensuring you get the best possible results for portraits, food photography, or close-up shots. You'll also benefit from AI enhancements that automatically improve color, brightness, and clarity for exceptional photo results.

Explore Your Creativity: Experiment with various shooting modes like portrait mode for professional-looking portraits with blurred backgrounds, night mode for capturing clear photos in low-light conditions, and macro mode for exploring the world of close-up photography. Additionally, the phone can record high-quality videos, allowing you to capture life's moments in stunning detail.

Power Throughout Your Day: Battery and Charging

Long-Lasting Endurance: Never get caught with a dead phone again. The Infinix Note 40 Pro/Pro+ packs a massive battery (likely 4600mAh for the Pro, 5000mAh for the Pro+) that can easily power you through a full day of use. Whether you're browsing the web, streaming videos, or gaming, this battery ensures you can stay connected and productive.

Charge Up in No Time: Even when the battery runs low, the phone's fast charging technology gets you back up and running quickly. The Pro+ model boasts impressive 100W fast charging, significantly reducing charging time. Imagine going from near empty to ready to go in just minutes! The Pro model might offer 45W fast charging, which is still significantly faster than traditional charging methods.

Wireless Freedom (if applicable): For ultimate convenience, some models might offer wireless charging capabilities. This allows you to simply place your phone on a compatible wireless charging pad to power

1.2 Package Contents

Get to know your new phone with a quick overview of its key features and design elements. Here's what you can expect to find in the box:

- The Star of the Show: Your Infinix Note 40 Pro/Pro+ smartphone in all its glory.
- Power Up: A charging adapter to keep your phone juiced up.
- Connecting Cable: A USB-C charging cable (or appropriate cable depending on region) to connect your phone to the adapter and your computer for data transfer (if applicable).
- SIM Card Ejector Tool: A small tool to help you safely remove the SIM card tray (if applicable to your model).
- Essential Guide: This user guide, packed with information to help you master your phone.
- Warranty Information: Documentation outlining the warranty coverage for your phone (may vary by region).

Optional Items:

Depending on your region or purchase option, you might also find some of these bonus items:

- Earphones: A pair of earphones for enjoying music, calls, and movies on the go.
- Pre-installed Screen Protector: A thin layer of plastic applied to the phone's screen to offer some protection from scratches during initial use (availability may vary).
- Protective Case: A case to provide additional protection for your phone against bumps and drops (availability may vary).

1.3 Inserting the SIM Card and microSD Card

What You'll Need:

- Your Infinix Note 40 Pro/Pro+ smartphone
- Your SIM card(s) (provided by your mobile carrier)
- A microSD card (optional, for expandable storage)
- The SIM card ejector tool (included in the box) (or a straightened paperclip)

Inserting the SIM Card(s):

1. Locate the SIM Card Tray: Look for a small hole on the side of your phone. This is where you'll insert the SIM card ejector tool. If you can't find the hole, consult the quick

start guide or user manual for specific instructions on your model.
2. **Eject the SIM Card Tray:** Gently push the ejector tool (or straightened paperclip) into the designated hole. You should feel a slight click, and the tray will pop out a bit. Carefully pull the tray out of the slot.
3. **Identify the SIM Slots**: Some phones have dual SIM slots, allowing you to use two different phone numbers or data plans. The tray might have markings indicating SIM 1 and SIM 2. Consult your user manual or carrier information for proper placement if you have a dual SIM phone.
4. **Place the SIM Card(s):** Hold the SIM card(s) with the gold contacts facing downwards. Carefully position the SIM card(s) in the designated slot(s) on the tray, matching the cutout shape.
5. **Insert the Tray Back In:** Once the SIM card(s) are securely placed, gently slide the tray back into the slot until it clicks into place.

Inserting a microSD Card:

1. Locate the microSD Card Slot: The microSD card slot might be on the SIM card tray or a separate slot on your phone. Refer to your user manual for the exact location.
2. Insert the microSD Card: Similar to the SIM card, hold the microSD card with the gold contacts facing downwards. Carefully align it with the cutout on the slot and gently push it in until it clicks into place.
3. Formatting the microSD Card (optional): Your phone might prompt you to format the microSD card before using it. Formatting erases any existing data, so ensure you have

a backup if necessary. Formatting optimizes the card for use with your phone.

1.4 Connecting to Wi-Fi

Let's connect your Infinix Note 40 Pro/Pro+ to the world wide web! Wi-Fi connectivity allows you to download apps, access online content, and stay connected with friends and family.

What You'll Need:

- Your Infinix Note 40 Pro/Pro+ smartphone
- The Wi-Fi network name (SSID) and password (if required)

Connecting to Wi-Fi:

1. Power On Your Phone: Press and hold the power button to turn on your phone.
2. Navigate to Wi-Fi Settings: During the initial setup process, you'll likely be prompted to connect to a Wi-Fi network. If you miss this step, you can access Wi-Fi settings manually. Here's a general guide, but the specific steps might vary slightly depending on your Android version:
   - Swipe down from the top of the screen to access the notification panel.
   - Locate the Wi-Fi icon (it might look like curved signal bars) and tap on it to hold or tap and hold for a few seconds to access the settings menu.

- Alternatively, you can access Settings > Network & internet (or Connections depending on your version).
3. **Select Your Wi-Fi Network:** You'll see a list of available Wi-Fi networks in your range. Choose the network you want to connect to.
4. **Enter the Password (if required):** If the network is password-protected, a pop-up window will appear requesting the password. Enter the Wi-Fi password for the chosen network and tap "Connect".
5. **Advanced Options (optional):** Some networks might have additional security features. You might see options like "Show password" or "WPA/WPA2/WPA3 Security". If you're unsure about these options, it's best to consult the network owner for assistance.
6. **Connected!** Once you enter the correct password (if required), your phone will attempt to connect to the Wi-Fi network. Upon successful connection, you'll see the Wi-Fi icon with full signal bars in the notification bar.

1.5 Creating a User Account

Here, we'll look at the two main options for creating a user account:

1. Setting Up a Google Account:

This is the most common option, granting access to a vast array of Google services and features:

- The Google Play Store: Download and install millions of apps, games, movies, music, and e-books.
- Gmail: Manage your email communication and stay connected.
- Google Drive: Store your photos, videos, documents, and other files securely in the cloud with 15GB of free storage (additional storage plans available for purchase).
- Google Photos: Organize and access your photos from any device.
- Google Maps: Navigate your world with ease.
- YouTube: Watch your favorite videos and creators.

Setting Up a Google Account:

- During the initial setup process, you'll be prompted to add a Google account.
- If you already have a Google account, enter your existing email address and password.
- If you don't have a Google account, you can easily create a new one directly on your phone by following the on-screen instructions.

2. Setting Up a Phone Manufacturer Account (if applicable):

Infinix might offer its own user account system with additional features or benefits specific to their devices. Here are some potential advantages:

- Cloud Storage: Infinix might offer its own cloud storage service for backing up your data or accessing exclusive content.

- Warranty Services: Registering your phone with an Infinix account might simplify warranty claims or provide access to support services.
- Customization Options: There could be Infinix-specific themes, wallpapers, or features accessible through their user account system.

Setting Up a Phone Manufacturer Account (if applicable):

- During setup or through the Settings menu, you might see an option to create an Infinix account.
- Follow the on-screen instructions to create a new account or link an existing one.

Choosing the Right Account:

For most users, setting up a Google account is the recommended option as it unlocks the vast ecosystem of Google services and apps. However, if Infinix offers compelling benefits with their user account system, you can consider creating one as well. It's ultimately up to your personal preference and needs.

1.6 Transferring Data from Your Old Phone

You are almost there! You've powered on your Infinix Note 40 Pro/Pro+, connected to Wi-Fi, and set up your user account. Now, let's tackle transferring your data from your old phone to your new one. This process ensures you don't lose important contacts, photos, videos, and other information during the switch.

There are several methods available to transfer data to your Infinix Note 40 Pro/Pro+, depending on your old phone's operating system and your preferences:

1. Using a Google Account: This is the simplest method for transferring data between Android phones. Here's what you'll need:

- Both phones connected to Wi-Fi.
- Your Google account credentials.

Transferring with Google Account:

1. During the initial setup on your Infinix Note 40 Pro/Pro+, choose the option to copy data from another phone.
2. Select "Android" as the old phone's operating system.
3. Sign in to your Google account on both your old and new phones.
4. You'll see a list of data transferable via your Google account, including contacts, calendar events, and some app data. Select the data you want to transfer.
5. Follow the on-screen instructions to complete the transfer process.

2. Using a Phone Clone App (if applicable):

Infinix might provide a pre-installed app specifically designed to transfer data between Infinix devices. This app can be a quicker and more comprehensive solution compared to using a Google account, potentially transferring additional data types like call history, messages, and even some app settings.

Transferring with a Phone Clone App:

1. Look for a pre-installed app named "Phone Clone" or similar on your Infinix Note 40 Pro/Pro+.
2. Launch the app and follow the on-screen instructions. You'll likely need to generate a QR code on your new phone and scan it with your old phone to establish a connection.
3. Select the data types you want to transfer and initiate the transfer process.

3. Transferring Data via Cable (if applicable):

Some phones, particularly older models, might offer the ability to transfer data directly using a cable connection. This method typically requires specific software or apps provided by your phone manufacturer.

Using a Cable for Transfer (if applicable):

1. Check your phone's user manuals or manufacturer's website to see if data transfer via cable is supported and what software or app is required.
2. Download and install the necessary software/app on both your old and new phones.

3. Connect the two phones using a compatible cable (refer to your user manuals for specific cable types).
4. Launch the data transfer software/app on both phones and follow the on-screen instructions to select and transfer your data.

4. Transferring Data Using a Cloud Storage Service:

Another option is to back up your data on a cloud storage service like Google Drive, Dropbox, or OneDrive and then restore it to your new phone.

Transferring with Cloud Storage:

1. Choose a cloud storage service you trust and ensure you have enough storage space for your data.
2. Back up your data (contacts, photos, videos, etc.) from your old phone to the chosen cloud storage service.
3. Install the cloud storage service app on your Infinix Note 40 Pro/Pro+ and log in to your account.
4. Locate the backed-up data and restore it to your new phone.

Choosing the Right Transfer Method:

The best transfer method depends on several factors, including:

- Your old phone's operating system (Android or iOS): Some methods are only compatible with Android devices.
- The amount of data you need to transfer: Cloud storage might be better for larger data volumes, while a cable connection could be faster for smaller transfers.
- Available features: Not all phones support data transfer via cable or have a pre-installed phone clone app.

Regardless of the method you choose, ensure both phones are fully charged or connected to a power source to avoid interruptions during the transfer process.

By following these steps, you can successfully transfer your data from your old phone to your new Infinix Note 40 Pro/Pro+ and get started with your new device without missing a beat!

Chapter 2: Getting to Know Your Phone

2.1 Physical Layout

Let's take a closer look at the Infinix Note 40 Pro/Pro+ physical design and button layout. Familiarizing yourself with the placements of various ports and buttons will allow you to navigate your phone with ease.

Front of the Phone:

- Large Display: The expansive display dominates the front, perfect for watching videos, gaming, and browsing the web.
- Front Camera (Punch-Hole or Waterdrop Notch): A small cutout (either a tiny hole or a teardrop-shaped notch) houses the front-facing camera for selfies and video calls. The exact location (centered or slightly off-center) might vary slightly depending on the model.
- Proximity Sensor (possible): An invisible sensor near the top bezel might be present to detect when your phone is close to your ear during calls, automatically turning off the display to save battery and prevent accidental screen touches.
- Ambient Light Sensor (possible): Another tiny sensor, often located near the top bezel or integrated within the front camera module, detects ambient light levels to automatically adjust the screen brightness for optimal viewing in different lighting conditions.

Back of the Phone:

- Rear Camera Module: The rear camera system is likely housed in a rectangular or square module protruding slightly from the back panel. The module will contain multiple lenses (likely including a main sensor, ultrawide sensor, and possibly others depending on the model) alongside an LED flash for low-light photography.
- Fingerprint Sensor (possible): Some models might integrate a fingerprint sensor for secure unlocking of the phone directly on the back panel. The sensor location could be near the center or slightly higher depending on the design.

Sides of the Phone:

- Power Button: The power button, also known as the side key, is typically located on the right side of the phone. It allows you to power on/off the device, lock/unlock the screen, and sometimes trigger additional functions with a long press (depending on your phone's settings).
- Volume Buttons: The volume buttons are usually located alongside the power button on the right side or on their own on the left side. These buttons allow you to control the media volume, ringtone volume, and notification volume.
- SIM Card Tray Slot: The SIM card tray slot for inserting your SIM card(s) might be found on the side of the phone. Refer to your user manual for the exact location and procedure for inserting/removing the SIM card tray.
- Microphone(s): Small microphone holes might be present on the bottom edge or other sides of the phone for capturing audio during calls, video recordings, and voice assistant interactions.

Top and Bottom of the Phone:

- USB-C Port: The universal USB-C port is most likely located at the bottom of the phone for charging the battery and transferring data to/from a computer.
- Speaker Grill(s): The speaker grilles for audio output (ringtones, music, games) might be located on the bottom edge or along the sides of the phone depending on the design.
- 3.5mm Headphone Jack (possible): Some models might retain a 3.5mm headphone jack for connecting wired headphones or earphones. The jack would typically be located on the top or bottom of the phone.

2.1.1 Buttons and Ports

Buttons:

- Power Button (Side Key):
    - Typically located on the right side of the phone.
    - Functions include:
        - Press and hold: Powers on/off the device.
        - Short press: Locks/unlocks the screen (if fingerprint unlock or PIN/password isn't enabled).
        - Long press (customizable): May trigger additional functions depending on your phone's settings, such as launching the Google Assistant or activating a power

menu with options for restart or emergency mode.
- Volume Buttons:
    - Location:
        - Usually alongside the power button on the right side.
        - Or, on their own on the left side.
    - Functions:
        - Increase or decrease media volume, ringtone volume, and notification volume.

Ports:

- USB-C Port:
    - Universal port located at the bottom of the phone for:
        - Charging the battery using a compatible power adapter.
        - Transferring data to/from a computer using a USB-C cable.
- 3.5mm Headphone Jack (possible):
    - Not all models might have this port.
    - If available, it's typically located on the top or bottom of the phone and allows you to connect wired headphones or earphones.

The SIM card tray slot for inserting your SIM card(s) is usually found on the side of the phone. Refer to your user manual for the exact location and procedure for inserting/removing the SIM card tray.

Microphone holes might be present on the bottom edge or other sides of the phone for capturing audio during calls, video recordings, and voice assistant interactions.

Speaker grilles for audio output (ringtones, music, games) might be located on the bottom edge or along the sides of the phone depending on the design.

2.1.2 Camera Layout

Rear Camera Module:

The rear camera module, likely located towards the top center or upper left corner of the back panel, houses all the camera lenses and a flash. Here's a breakdown of the typical components you might find:

- Main Sensor: This is the primary camera lens, usually boasting the highest megapixel count (likely 108MP on the Pro+, 48MP on the Pro) and responsible for capturing most of your everyday photos and videos.
- Ultrawide Sensor (possible): Many phones include an ultrawide sensor that allows you to capture expansive landscapes, group photos in tight spaces, or add a dramatic effect to your photos by fitting more of the scene into the frame.
- Depth Sensor (possible): Some models might have a depth sensor that assists with capturing bokeh effects (blurred backgrounds) in portrait mode photos.
- LED Flash: An LED flash provides illumination for low-light photography and videography.

Identifying Your Specific Lenses:

While the above layout is typical, the exact combination of lenses might vary slightly depending on your specific Infinix Note 40 Pro/Pro+ model. Refer to your user manual or product specifications to confirm the exact lenses and megapixel counts on your device.

Here are some additional details to help you identify the lenses on your phone:

- Size and Placement: The main sensor is usually the largest lens within the camera module.
- Ultrawide Lens: The ultrawide lens might have markings or an icon indicating its purpose. It could also be slightly wider than the other lenses.

Remember: Regardless of the specific lens combination, your camera app will provide options for selecting different shooting modes, allowing you to leverage the strengths of each lens and capture beautiful photos under various conditions.

2.1.3 Fingerprint Sensor

Locating the Fingerprint Sensor:

The fingerprint sensor might be integrated in different locations depending on the design of your specific model. Here are the common placements:

- Rear-Mounted Sensor: This is the most typical location. Look for a designated fingerprint sensor area on the back panel, usually towards the lower center or slightly higher.
- In-Display Sensor (possible): Some advanced models might incorporate an in-display fingerprint sensor. If present, you'll see a fingerprint icon on the lower portion of the display where you need to place your finger to unlock the phone.

Checking for a Fingerprint Sensor:

The easiest way to confirm if your phone has a fingerprint sensor is to swipe down from the notification panel and look for a shortcut or setting related to fingerprints. If you see options like "Fingerprint sensor" or "Fingerprint unlock," then your phone has this feature.

Setting Up Fingerprint Unlock:

If your phone has a fingerprint sensor and you want to use it for unlocking, you'll need to set it up during the initial phone setup or through the Settings menu. Here's a general guideline, but the specific steps might vary slightly depending on your Android version:

1. Access Settings > Security (or Lock screen depending on your version).
2. Look for the Fingerprint unlock option and tap on it.
3. You might be prompted to enter your current lock screen PIN, password, or pattern (if already set).
4. Follow the on-screen instructions to carefully place your finger on the fingerprint sensor repeatedly at different angles to capture a complete fingerprint scan.

5. You might be able to add multiple fingerprints for increased security or convenience (adding fingers for different hands).

Once you've successfully set up fingerprint unlock, you can simply place your finger on the sensor to wake and unlock your phone. Fingerprint unlock offers a secure and faster alternative to PINs, passwords, or patterns.

2.2 Home Screen and App Drawer

2.2.1 Navigating the Home Screen

The home screen is your central hub for interacting with your Infinix Note 40 Pro/Pro+. It's the first screen you encounter when you turn on or unlock your phone, and it provides a customizable canvas to organize your favorite apps, widgets, and shortcuts for quick access. Let's navigate and personalize your home screen.

Understanding the Layout:

- Home Screen Pages: Your home screen stretches across multiple pages, accessible by swiping left or right. You can add or remove home screen pages as needed.

- Dock: The dock sits at the bottom of your home screen and typically holds 4-5 app icons for quick access to your most-used applications.
- Wallpaper: The background image behind your app icons and widgets.

Customizing Your Home Screen:

- Setting Wallpaper:
    1. Long tap on an empty space on the home screen.
    2. Tap on "Wallpaper" or "Wallpapers" (depending on your device).
    3. Choose your desired wallpaper source (pre-loaded wallpapers, live wallpapers, or your own photos).
    4. Select the image you want to use and crop it to fit the screen if necessary.
    5. Tap "Set wallpaper" or similar to apply the wallpaper.
- Adding Widgets:
    1. Long tap on an empty space on the home screen to enter the widget selection menu.
    2. Browse the available widgets. These might include weather, calendar, music player, contacts, or app-specific widgets.
    3. Tap and hold on a desired widget to enter edit mode.
    4. Drag the widget to a preferred spot on the home screen and release your finger to place it.
- Arranging App Icons:
    1. Tap and hold on an app icon until it enters edit mode (wiggles or displays a menu).

2. Drag and drop the app icon to a new location on the current home screen page or another home screen page (accessible by swiping left/right).
3. You can also drag app icons on top of other app icons to create folders for better organization.

- Adding Apps to the Home Screen:
    1. Access the app drawer by swiping up from the bottom of the home screen (typical gesture).
    2. Find the app you want to add to the home screen.
    3. Tap and hold on the app icon until it enters edit mode.
    4. Drag the app icon to the desired location on one of your home screen pages and release your finger to place it.
- Removing Apps from the Home Screen:
    1. Tap and hold on an app icon until it enters edit mode (wiggles or displays a menu).
    2. Some devices display an "X" or "Remove" option on the top corner of the app icon. Drag the app icon to this option and release your finger to remove it from the home screen (the app itself is not uninstalled from the phone).
- Customizing the Dock:
    1. You can add, remove, or rearrange apps in the dock using the same method as arranging app icons on the home screen (tap, hold, drag, and drop).
    2. The ability to add or remove apps from the dock itself might vary depending on your launcher.

Navigation Tips:

- Swiping Up: Accesses the app drawer (usually).

- Swiping Left/Right: Navigates between home screen pages.
- Tapping and Holding on an App Icon: Enters edit mode for moving or uninstalling (from home screen) the app.
- Tapping on an App Icon: Launches the corresponding application.

By following these steps, you can personalize your Infinix Note 40 Pro/Pro+ home screen to match your preferences and keep your most-used apps, widgets, and shortcuts within easy reach.

2.2.2 Adding, Removing, and Organizing Apps

Adding Apps to the Home Screen:

1. Access the App Drawer: Swipe up from the bottom of your home screen (typical gesture) to open the app drawer, which houses all the apps installed on your phone.
2. Locate the Desired App: Browse through the app drawer or use the search bar at the top (if available) to find the app you want to add to your home screen.
3. Drag and Drop the App Icon: Tap and hold on the app icon until it enters edit mode (usually indicated by wiggling icons or a menu). Then, drag the app icon to a preferred spot on one of your home screen pages and release your finger to place it.

Removing Apps from the Home Screen:

1. Enter Edit Mode: Tap and hold on an app icon on your home screen until it enters edit mode (wiggles or displays a menu).
2. Locate the Remove Option:
    - Some devices display an "X" or "Remove" option on the top corner of the app icon. Drag the app icon to this option and release your finger to remove it from the home screen.
    - Alternatively, you might need to drag the app icon to a specific area on the screen, such as "Remove" or "Uninstall" zone (if available on your launcher).
3. Confirmation (Optional): Some launchers might prompt you for confirmation before removing the app from the home screen. Tap "Remove" or "OK" to confirm the removal.

Remember: Removing an app from the home screen only removes the shortcut, not the app itself. The app will still be installed on your phone and accessible through the app drawer.

Organizing Apps for Efficiency:

- Grouping Related Apps: Create folders to group similar apps together. This helps declutter your home screen and keep things organized. To create a folder, simply drag and drop one app icon on top of another. You can rename the folder by tapping on it and entering a new name.
- Arranging Apps by Frequency: Place the apps you use most often on the primary home screen page for quick access. Less-used apps can reside on secondary home screen pages.
- Utilizing the Dock: The dock at the bottom of your home screen provides quick access to a few favorite apps.

Experiment and find the arrangement that works best for you.

2.2.3 Accessing the App Drawer

The app drawer on your Infinix Note 40 Pro/Pro+ is a central location that houses all the applications installed on your device. It serves as your library, allowing you to access any app on your phone, regardless of whether it's added to the home screen or not.

Locating the App Drawer:

There are two common ways to access the app drawer on most Android phones:

- Swipe Up Gesture (Typical Method):
    1. Navigate to your home screen.
    2. Swipe up from the bottom of the home screen with your finger. This gesture is similar to how you might flick upwards to unlock the phone on some models.
- App Drawer Button (Less Common):
    1. Some phone launchers might have a dedicated app drawer button on the home screen itself. This button is usually located along the bottom edge of the screen but could vary depending on your specific launcher.
    2. If your phone has an app drawer button, simply tap on it to open the app drawer.

Whichever method you use, swiping up from the bottom of the home screen is the most common way to access the app drawer on Android phones.

Navigating the App Drawer:

- Browse by Category (Possible): Some app drawers might categorize apps into groups (Social, Entertainment, Productivity, etc.) for easier browsing.
- Alphabetical List: If not categorized, the app drawer will likely display all apps in an alphabetical list.
- Search Bar: Most app drawers include a search bar at the top. Utilize this bar to quickly find a specific app by name.

Once you've located the desired app in the app drawer, simply tap on its icon to launch the application.

Remember: You can add frequently used apps to your home screen for quicker access, while the app drawer serves as a comprehensive list of all installed apps on your Infinix Note 40 Pro/Pro+. By effectively using both the home screen and app drawer, you can organize your apps and keep your phone clutter-free.

2.3 Notifications Panel

2.3.1 Accessing Notifications

There are two main ways to access your notifications:

1. Swiping Down from the Status Bar:
   - The status bar is located at the top of your screen and usually displays the time, battery level, signal strength, and notification icons.
   - Swipe down from the status bar with your finger to reveal the notification panel.
2. Using a Second Swipe (Possible):
   - On some Infinix models or depending on your launcher settings, you might need to swipe down twice from the status bar to fully expand the notification panel and view all your notification details.

Understanding the Notification Panel:

- Notification Icons: You'll see icons representing the apps that have sent you notifications.
- Notification Previews: Depending on your app settings and Android version, you might see a short preview of the notification content (e.g., a new message snippet or social media update).
- Action Buttons (Possible): Some notifications might have buttons allowing you to perform quick actions directly from the notification panel, such as replying to a message or dismissing an alarm.

Interacting with Notifications:

- Opening a Notification: Tap on a notification to open the relevant app and view the full notification details.
- Clearing a Notification: Swipe the notification to the side (usually left or right) to dismiss it.

- Clearing All Notifications: Tap on "Clear All" (or similar wording) located at the bottom of the notification panel to dismiss all notifications at once.

Accessing Notification Settings:

- Tap and Hold the Settings Cog (Optional):
    1. Swiping down twice from the status bar might reveal a settings cog icon in the notification panel. Tap and hold on this icon to access notification settings for all your apps.
- Accessing Settings Menu:
    1. Swipe down the notification panel.
    2. Swipe down again to fully expand it if necessary (depending on your model).
    3. Look for a "Settings" option or tap on the three dots (...) menu (if available) and locate a "Settings" or "Notification settings" option. This will open the notification settings menu.

Notification Settings Menu:

The notification settings menu allows you to control how and when you receive notifications for each app. You can:

- Turn Off Notifications Completely: Disable notifications for an app entirely.
- Choose Notification Style: Select how you want notifications to appear (sound, vibration, pop-up banner, etc.).
- Set Notification Priority: Prioritize notifications from important apps so they don't get buried by less important ones.

By understanding how to access and manage your notifications, you can stay informed about what matters while maintaining control over how alerts are delivered on your Infinix Note 40 Pro/Pro+.

2.3.2 Clearing Notifications

There are three main ways to clear notifications on your Infinix Note 40 Pro/Pro+:

- Clearing Individual Notifications:
    1. Swipe down from the status bar to open the notification panel.
    2. Locate the notification you want to dismiss.
    3. Swipe the notification to the side (usually left or right) to clear it.
- Clearing All Notifications:
    1. Swipe down from the status bar to open the notification panel.
    2. Locate a "Clear All" option (or similar wording) at the bottom of the notification panel.
    3. Tap on "Clear All" to dismiss all your notifications at once.
- Clearing Notifications from the Lock Screen (Possible):
    1. Double-swipe down from the status bar on the lock screen (similar to unlocking the phone) to expand the notification panel.
    2. Swipe individual notifications away or tap "Clear All" to dismiss all notifications.

Note: On some Infinix models, you might need to swipe down twice from the lock screen to fully reveal the notification panel with clear functionality.

Additional Tips:

- Notification Settings: Explore the notification settings menu (accessible by swiping down twice on the notification panel and tapping "Settings" or similar) to manage app-specific notification behavior. You can choose to turn off notifications entirely for specific apps or silence them for a period.
- Do Not Disturb Mode: Utilize Do Not Disturb mode when you need to focus or avoid distractions. This mode silences notifications and calls (with customization options available).

2.3.3 Customizing Notification Settings

Accessing Notification Settings:

There are two main ways to access notification settings on most Android phones:

1. Swiping Down Twice and Tapping "Settings" (Typical Method):

1. Swipe down from the status bar twice to fully expand the notification panel.
2. Locate a "Settings" cog icon or tap on three dots (...) menu (if available) in the notification panel.
3. Tap on "Settings" or "Notification settings" to access the notification settings menu.
2. Accessing Settings Menu:
    1. Open the Settings app on your Infinix Note 40 Pro/Pro+.
    2. Look for a section labelled "Notifications" or "Sounds & notifications" (depending on your device). Tap on that section to access the notification settings menu.

Customizing Notification Settings:

The notification settings menu grants you granular control over how you receive notifications for each app installed on your device. Here's what you can typically adjust:

- App Notifications: Toggle notifications on or off entirely for individual apps.
- Notification Style: Choose how you want notifications to appear: sound, vibration, pop-up banner, or silently appear in the notification panel without any interruptions.
- Notification Priority: Set priority levels for app notifications. Urgent notifications from important apps (like messages or calls) can bypass Do Not Disturb mode if set as priorities.
- App Settings (Possible): Some apps might have their own notification settings within their app settings menu. You can access these by going into the app's settings and finding the notification section.

Utilizing Notification Settings Effectively:

- Prioritize Important Apps: Ensure notifications from critical apps (messages, emails, calls) make noise or display pop-up banners to stay informed.
- Silence Less Urgent Apps: Turn off notifications for less important apps (games, social media) or choose silent notification styles (no sound or vibration) to avoid distractions.
- Do Not Disturb Mode: Schedule Do Not Disturb mode for times when you need focus or want to avoid interruptions. You can customize Do Not Disturb mode to allow notifications from specific contacts or apps while silencing others.

2.4 Quick Settings Panel

Accessing the Quick Settings Panel:

There are two common ways to access the Quick Settings Panel:

- Swiping Down Once (Typical Method):
    1. Swipe down from the top of your screen with one finger. This motion reveals the first few quick setting tiles.
- Swiping Down Twice (Possible):

1. On some Infinix models, you might need to swipe down twice from the top of the screen to fully expand the Quick Settings Panel and view all available options.

Understanding the Quick Settings Panel:

- Quick Setting Tiles: The Quick Settings Panel displays a grid of square or rectangular icons representing various settings and features. Tapping a tile toggles the setting on or off (e.g., Wi-Fi, Bluetooth).
- Brightness Slider (Possible): Some Quick Settings Panels might include a brightness slider allowing you to adjust the screen brightness without going into the Settings menu.
- Notification Panel Access: Swiping down further from the expanded Quick Settings Panel usually transitions you to the notification panel, where you can view all your app notifications.

Common Quick Settings Tiles (Icons may vary):

- Wi-Fi
- Bluetooth
- Location
- Do Not Disturb
- Sound Mode (Silent, Vibrate, Ring)
- Screen Rotation
- Flashlight
- Battery Saver
- Cast (Miracast)
- Data Saver

Customizing the Quick Settings Panel:

- Editing the Tiles (Possible): Most Infinix devices allow you to customize the icons displayed in the Quick Settings Panel. Look for an "Edit" or "Customize" button (usually a pencil icon) within the Quick Settings Panel. Tapping this button will allow you to:
    - Drag and rearrange existing tiles to position frequently used functions for quicker access.
    - Add new tiles by dragging them from a hidden list to the main panel.
    - Remove tiles you don't use often.

Benefits of Using the Quick Settings Panel:

- Quick Access: The Quick Settings Panel eliminates the need to delve into the Settings app for frequently used functions.
- Customization: You can tailor the Quick Settings Panel to include the features you use most often, making it a personalized shortcut to your preferred settings.

By understanding and customizing the Quick Settings Panel on your Infinix Note 40 Pro/Pro+, you can enhance your device's usability and control essential settings with a few swipes and taps.

Part 2: Essential Features

Chapter 3: Making and Receiving Calls

3.1 Using the Dial Pad

The Dial Pad, also known as the Phone app, is your gateway to making phone calls and accessing other calling features on your Infinix Note 40 Pro/Pro+. This section will guide you through using the Dial Pad for efficient communication.

Launching the Dial Pad:

There are two main ways to launch the Dial Pad app:

- Phone App Icon: Locate the Phone app icon on your home screen or app drawer. This icon is usually a universal phone symbol. Tap on the icon to launch the Dial Pad.
- Speed Dial (Possible): Some Infinix models might allow you to program specific contacts for speed dialing from the lock screen or standby screen. Refer to your user manual or explore the Phone app settings to see if your device supports this feature.

Using the Dial Pad:

The Dial Pad displays a layout similar to a traditional landline phone with numbers (0-9), symbols (* and #), and buttons for call initiation and call history access. Here's how to make a call using the Dial Pad:

1. Enter the Phone Number: Tap on the number keys on the Dial Pad to enter the phone number you want to call.
2. Initiate the Call: Once you've entered the number, tap on the "Call" button (usually a green phone icon) located at the bottom of the Dial Pad screen to initiate the call.

Additional Dial Pad Features:

- Backspace: The backspace button (usually an arrow pointing left) allows you to erase digits you entered accidentally.
- Speed Dial (Possible): As mentioned earlier, some Infinix models might allow you to assign specific contacts to specific numbers on the Dial Pad for speed dialing. Refer to your user manual or explore the Phone app settings for details on setting up speed dial.
- Call History: The Dial Pad might have a "Recent" or "Call History" tab that displays a list of recently dialed, received, and missed calls. You can tap on a number in the call history to redial the contact.
- Dial Pad Options (Possible): Some Infinix phones might have additional options accessible through a menu button (usually three dots (...) or a menu icon) on the Dial Pad screen. These options might include:
    - Accessing voicemail.

- Adding a contact (if the number you dialed is not already saved in your contacts).
  - Searching your contacts list.

Using the Dial Pad Effectively:

- Save Contacts: Save frequently called numbers in your phone's contacts list for easier access. You can access the contacts list through a dedicated Contacts app or through the Phone app itself (depending on your device).
- Speed Dial (if available): Utilize speed dial for frequently contacted individuals to save time dialing numbers manually.
- Call History: The call history can be helpful for redialing missed calls or reconnecting with someone you spoke to recently.

3.2 Making Calls

Activating the Dial Pad:

There are two primary ways to activate the Dial Pad app:

- Phone App Icon: Locate the Phone app icon on your home screen or app drawer. This icon is usually a universal phone symbol. Tap on the icon to launch the Dial Pad.
- Speed Dial (Possible): Some Infinix models might allow you to program specific contacts for speed dialing from the lock screen or standby screen. Refer to your user manual or explore the Phone app settings to see if your device supports this feature.

Using the Dial Pad:

The Dial Pad resembles a traditional phone with a keypad containing numbers (0-9), symbols (* and #), and buttons for initiating calls and accessing call history. Here's how to make a call using the Dial Pad:

1. Enter the Phone Number: Tap on the number keys on the Dial Pad to input the phone number you want to call.
2. Initiate the Call: Once you've entered the number, tap on the "Call" button (usually a green phone icon) located at the bottom of the Dial Pad screen to initiate the call.

Additional Dial Pad Features:

- Backspace: The backspace button (usually an arrow pointing left) allows you to erase digits you entered accidentally.
- Speed Dial (Possible): As mentioned earlier, some Infinix models might allow assigning specific contacts to specific numbers on the Dial Pad for speed dialing. Refer to your user manual or explore the Phone app settings for details on setting up speed dial.
- Call History: The Dial Pad might have a "Recent" or "Call History" tab that displays a list of recently dialed, received, and missed calls. You can tap on a number in the call history to redial the contact.
- Dial Pad Options (Possible): Some Infinix phones might have additional options accessible through a menu button (usually three dots (...) or a menu icon) on the Dial Pad screen. These options might include:
    - Accessing voicemail.

- o Adding a contact (if the number you dialed is not already saved in your contacts).
- o Searching your contacts list.

Making Calls Effectively:

- Save Contacts: Save frequently called numbers in your phone's contacts list for easier access. You can access the contacts list through a dedicated Contacts app or through the Phone app itself (depending on your device).
- Speed Dial (if available): Utilize speed dial for frequently contacted individuals to save time dialing numbers manually.
- Call History: The call history can be helpful for redialing missed calls or reconnecting with someone you spoke to recently.

Beyond the Dial Pad - Additional Calling Features:

- Contacts App: The Contacts app stores your contact information, including names, phone numbers, email addresses, and notes. You can use the Contacts app to find and call a contact directly.
- Favorites (Possible): Some Phone apps allow you to create a Favorites list for quick access to your most important contacts.
- In-Call Features: During a call, you'll typically see options to mute the microphone, put the call on hold, activate speakerphone, or access additional functions depending on your carrier and device.

3.3 Receiving Calls

Recognizing Incoming Calls:

- Ringtone and Vibration: When you receive a call, your phone will play your designated ringtone and might vibrate (depending on your settings) to notify you of the incoming call.
- Caller ID (if available): The phone screen will usually display information about the incoming caller, such as their name (if saved in your contacts) or phone number.

Answering Calls:

- Swipe to Answer: When the call comes in, you'll see a slide or swipe answer prompt on the screen (usually a green colored button or icon). Swipe your finger across the answer prompt towards the right side of the screen to answer the call.
- Answer Button (Possible): Some Infinix models might display an "Answer" button instead of a swipe gesture. Tap on the "Answer" button to pick up the call.

Declining Calls:

- Swipe to Decline: If you don't want to answer the call, you can swipe your finger across the answer prompt on the screen (usually a red colored button or icon) towards the left side of the screen to decline the call.
- Decline Button (Possible): Some Infinix models might display a "Decline" button instead of a swipe gesture. Tap on the "Decline" button to reject the call.

Additional Options During Incoming Calls:

- Caller Options (Possible): During the incoming call screen, you might see additional options depending on your device and Android version. These options might include:
    - Silencing the ringer without declining the call.
    - Sending a text message to the caller (e.g., letting them know you can't answer right now).

Customizing Call Settings:

- Ringtones and Sounds: You can customize your ringtones and notification sounds within the Settings menu of your Infinix Note 40 Pro/Pro+. This allows you to personalize how your phone alerts you of incoming calls and notifications.
- Vibration: You can enable or disable vibration for incoming calls within the Settings menu.
- Call Forwarding (Possible): Your carrier might offer call forwarding features that allow you to divert incoming calls to voicemail or another phone number under certain conditions. You can typically manage call forwarding settings through your carrier's online account or by contacting customer service.

3.4 Call History

Understanding Call History:

Your call history typically displays a list of your recent calls, categorized by:

- Missed Calls: These calls will usually have a missed call icon or the word "Missed" displayed next to the contact information.
- Outgoing Calls: These calls you initiated will have a notation indicating the outgoing nature of the call.
- Received Calls: These calls that came into your phone will be displayed without any missed call or outgoing icons.

Each call entry might also provide details such as:

- Contact Name (if available): If the number is saved in your contacts list, the call history will display the caller's name.
- Phone Number: The phone number of the caller will be displayed.
- Call Time and Date: You'll see the time and date the call occurred.
- Call Duration (Possible): Some call history entries might show the duration of the call.

Interacting with Call History:

- Tapping on a Call Entry: Tapping on a call entry in your history might allow you to:
    - Return the call by dialing the number again.
    - View additional information about the call (if available).
    - Add the number to your contacts list (if it's not already saved).
    - Delete the call history entry.

Managing Call History:

- Deleting Individual Entries: Tap and hold on a call history entry to select it. You might then see a delete option or a menu allowing you to delete the call entry.
- Clearing All Call History (Possible): Some Phone apps might offer an option to clear your entire call history at once. Look for a "Clear Call History" option within the call history menu or the Phone app settings.

Utilizing Call History:

- Missed Calls: Your call history allows you to see missed calls and return them if necessary.
- Recalling Recent Calls: You can easily find and redial numbers you've spoken to recently through your call history.
- Managing Contacts: The call history can help you identify frequently called numbers that you might want to add to your contacts list for easier communication in the future.

By understanding and managing your call history on your Infinix Note 40 Pro/Pro+, you can stay on top of your communications and ensure you never miss an important follow-up.

3.5 Voicemail and Call Forwarding

Even with the best planning, there will be times when you can't answer your phone. This section will look at two voicemail and call forwarding features (if applicable to your carrier) on your Infinix Note 40 Pro/Pro+ to ensure you never miss important messages:

1. Voicemail:

Voicemail is a service offered by most mobile carriers that allows callers to leave a message when you can't answer your phone. Here's how to access and manage voicemail on your Infinix Note 40 Pro/Pro+ (specific steps might vary slightly depending on your carrier):

- Checking Voicemail:
    - Option 1: Direct Dial (Universal): This method works for most carriers. Dial your voicemail number (usually pre-programmed into your phone as "Voicemail" or a specific number provided by your carrier) to access your voicemail messages directly.
    - Option 2: Phone App (Possible): Some Phone apps might have a built-in voicemail tab or option. Explore your Phone app's menus or settings to see if this functionality is available.
- Listening to Voicemail Messages:
    - Once you've accessed your voicemail system, follow the prompts to navigate your voicemail

inbox. You'll typically be able to listen to new messages, saved messages, and even delete messages you don't need.
- Customizing Voicemail (Possible):
  o Your voicemail system might allow you to personalize your voicemail greeting, which is the message callers hear when you don't answer. You might also be able to set notification options for new voicemail messages. Consult your carrier's instructions or voicemail system prompts for details on available customization features.

2. Call Forwarding (if applicable):

Call forwarding is a feature (offered by most carriers) that allows you to redirect incoming calls to another phone number under certain conditions. Here are some common call forwarding options (availability may depend on your carrier):

- Forward Always: This diverts all incoming calls to a designated number.
- Forward When Busy: This forwards calls only when your line is busy or you don't answer after a certain number of rings.
- Forward When Unreachable: This forwards calls when your phone is turned off or out of signal range.

Activating and Deactivating Call Forwarding (if applicable):

- Call forwarding is typically managed through service codes provided by your carrier. These codes can be dialed like regular phone numbers to activate or deactivate specific call forwarding options. You might also be able to manage call forwarding through your carrier's online account or mobile app (if available).

Important Note: Call forwarding might incur additional charges depending on your carrier plan. Be sure to consult your carrier's website or customer service for details on voicemail and call forwarding features, including any associated costs.

Chapter 4: Text Messaging (SMS/MMS)

4.1 Sending and Receiving Text Messages

Understanding SMS and MMS:

- SMS:
    - Stands for Short Message Service.
    - Primarily used for sending plain text messages.
    - Limited to approximately 160 characters per message (depending on your carrier and character encoding).
    - Ideal for quick updates, short conversations, or sending quick information.
- MMS:
    - Stands for Multimedia Messaging Service.
    - Allows you to send and receive multimedia content along with text in your messages.
    - This multimedia content can include pictures, videos, and even audio recordings.
    - MMS messages are larger than SMS and might be subject to data charges depending on your carrier plan.

Sending SMS and MMS Messages:

1. Open the Messaging App: Locate and tap on the Messaging app icon on your home screen or app drawer. This app is usually represented by a text message icon or the word "Messages".
2. Start a New Conversation or Compose:
    - New Conversation: You can initiate a new text message conversation by tapping on the "New message" icon (usually a plus sign (+) or a text bubble icon) in the Messaging app. This will open a new message screen.
    - Replying to an Existing Conversation: If you're responding to an existing message thread, simply tap on the conversation you want to reply to from your message list.
3. Enter Recipient(s): In the "To" field, enter the phone number(s) of the person or people you want to send the message to. You can add multiple recipients by separating their numbers with commas.
4. Compose Your Message:
    - SMS: Simply type your message in the text input field at the bottom of the screen.
    - MMS: To add multimedia content, tap on the picture or paperclip attachment icon and select the photos, videos, or audio recordings you want to send. You can usually compose a text message alongside the multimedia content in the same message.
5. Sending the Text Message: Once you've composed your message, tap on the "Send" icon (usually an arrow pointing upwards) located in the text input field or beside the recipient field to send the message.

Distinguishing Between SMS and MMS Sending:

- Automatic Conversion (Possible): If you exceed the character limit for an SMS message while composing and your phone has an MMS plan, the Messaging app might automatically convert the message to MMS to accommodate the extra content. You might see a notification or icon indicating this conversion.

Receiving SMS and MMS Messages:

- Text messages are received through the Messaging app.
- When a new message arrives, you'll typically hear a notification sound and see a notification appear on your screen, depending on your settings.
- Tapping on the notification or opening the Messaging app will allow you to view the new message and respond if desired.
- SMS messages will appear as plain text, while MMS messages might display a thumbnail preview of the included picture or multimedia content.

Additional Considerations:

- MMS and Data Charges: Sending and receiving MMS messages use your mobile data plan. Be sure you have a data plan that supports your texting habits if you plan to send MMS messages frequently.
- Carrier Compatibility: MMS messaging might not be compatible with all carriers or phones. Ensure both you and

the recipient have MMS enabled on your plans for successful multimedia message exchange.

4.2 Adding Attachments (Photos, Videos)

While SMS excels for quick text-based communication, MMS (Multimedia Messaging Service) on your Infinix Note 40 Pro/Pro+ allows you to add richness and personality to your messages by incorporating photos and videos.

This section will guide you through adding attachments to your text messages.

Prerequisites for Sending MMS:

- MMS-Compatible Carrier Plan: Ensure your mobile carrier plan supports MMS messaging. Data charges typically apply to MMS usage.
- Recipient Compatibility: MMS messaging might not be compatible with all carriers or phones. Verify if the recipient has an MMS-enabled plan to ensure they can receive your multimedia messages.

Attaching Photos and Videos to Text Messages:

1. Launch the Messaging App: Locate and tap on the Messaging app icon on your home screen or app drawer.
2. Start a New Conversation or Compose:

- New Conversation: You can initiate a new text message conversation by tapping on the "New message" icon (usually a plus sign (+) or a text bubble icon) in the Messaging app. This will open a new message screen.
- Replying to an Existing Conversation: If you're responding to an existing message thread, simply tap on the conversation you want to reply to from your message list.
3. Enter Recipient(s): In the "To" field, enter the phone number(s) of the person or people you want to send the message to. You can add multiple recipients by separating their numbers with commas.
4. Compose your Text Message (Optional): You can include a text message along with your photos or videos.
5. Attaching Multimedia Content:
    - Tap on the picture or paperclip attachment icon in the message compose field. This icon usually appears beside the text input field.
    - A menu might appear with options to select photos, videos, or even audio recordings. Choose the appropriate option based on the type of attachment you want to add.
6. Selecting Photos or Videos:
    - Depending on your selection in step 5, you'll be directed to your gallery, photos app, or video app.
    - Browse and select the photo or video you want to attach to your message.
    - You might be able to select multiple photos or videos depending on your Messaging app's capabilities and your carrier's MMS limitations.
7. Compose and Send:

- After selecting your attachments, you'll be returned to the message compose screen where you can preview your attached content.
- You can add a text message to accompany your attachments if desired.
- Once you've finished composing your message, tap on the "Send" icon (usually an arrow pointing upwards) to send the MMS message.

Additional Considerations:

- Image and Video Size Limits: MMS messages have size limitations. If your photos or videos are too large, you might need to compress them before sending using your gallery app or a third-party photo editing app.
- Data Usage: MMS messages use your mobile data plan. Be mindful of data usage charges, especially if you frequently send MMS messages.

4.3 Managing Conversations

Viewing Conversations:

- Conversation List: When you open the Messaging app, you'll see a list of your existing text message conversations.
- Individual Conversations: Each conversation in the list represents an exchange with a specific contact or group of contacts. Tapping on a conversation will open it, displaying the message history between you and the recipient(s).

Navigating Conversations:

- Scrolling Through Messages: Swipe up or down on the conversation screen to view the message history. Newer messages will be displayed towards the bottom of the screen.
- Viewing Timestamps: Each message will typically have a timestamp indicating the date and time the message was sent or received.

Conversing with Multiple People:

- Group Chats: The Messaging app allows you to create group chats where you can exchange messages with multiple people at once. Group message threads are denoted by the names or numbers of all participants in the group.

Managing Individual Conversations:

- Starred Conversations (Possible): Some Messaging apps allow you to "star" important conversations to prioritize them in your conversation list. Tapping on a starred conversation icon (usually a star icon) next to a conversation might add it to your starred list for easier access.
- Pinning Conversations (Possible): Some Messaging apps allow you to "pin" conversations to the top of your conversation list for quick access. Tapping on a pin icon (usually a pin icon) next to a conversation might pin it to the top of your list.

Bulk Conversation Management (Possible):

- Deleting Conversations: You can typically delete unwanted conversations from your conversation list. Selecting a conversation and tapping on a "Delete" option (usually a trash can icon) might delete the conversation thread.
- Deleting Multiple Conversations (Possible): Some Messaging apps might offer the ability to delete multiple conversations at once. Look for a "Delete" option while selecting multiple conversations (usually by tapping and holding on a conversation to select it and then selecting other conversations to delete).

Search (Possible):

- Some Messaging apps have a built-in search function that allows you to search through your message history for specific keywords or contact names.

Organizing Conversations with Tools (Possible):

- Some Messaging apps offer features like labels or tags that you can assign to conversations to categorize them for easier searching and organization.

4.4 Blocking Numbers

There might be times when you want to block unwanted calls or text messages from specific numbers. Your Infinix Note 40 Pro/Pro+ provides you with the ability to block such numbers, giving you control over your communication experience.

Blocking Methods (Possible):

There are two main ways to block numbers on your Infinix Note 40 Pro/Pro+:

- Using the Phone App: You can block numbers directly from the Phone app's call history or through the contact information of the number you want to block.
- Using the Messaging App (Possible): Some Messaging apps might allow you to block numbers directly from a message thread.

Blocking Through the Phone App:

1. Access Call History or Contact Information:
    - Call History: Locate and launch the Phone app. Navigate to your call history tab (usually called "Recent" or "Call History"). Find the entry for the number you want to block.
    - Contact Information: If the number you want to block is saved in your contacts, open the contact's information page within the Contacts app or Phone app.
2. Locate the Block Option:
    - Call History: While viewing the call history entry for the number you want to block, look for a "Block" option, "Block number," or a similar menu option. This option might be displayed next to the number or through a menu button (usually three dots (...) or a menu icon).
    - Contact Information: While viewing the contact information for the number you want to block, look for a "Block" option, "Block number," or a similar

menu option. This option might be located near the contact's name or phone number or through a menu button.
3. Confirm Blocking:
    o Tapping the "Block" option or confirmation message will typically block the selected number. You might see a confirmation message prompting you to confirm your action.

Blocking Through the Messaging App (if applicable):

1. Open the Message Thread: Locate and open the message thread from the number you want to block.
2. Locate the Block Option (Possible): Some Messaging apps might have a "Block" option or similar menu option within the message thread. This option might be located next to the sender's name or information or through a menu button.
3. Confirm Blocking (if applicable): Tapping the "Block" option or confirmation message might block the number from messaging you again.

Important Notes:

- The specific steps to block numbers might vary slightly depending on your Android version and phone model. Consult your user manual or explore the Phone and Messaging apps for their specific blocking functionalities.
- Blocking a number only blocks communication from that specific number. If someone is harassing you from multiple numbers, you might need to block each number individually.
- Blocking calls or messages won't necessarily delete past conversations or call history entries from that number.

Chapter 5: Managing Contacts

5.1 Adding and Editing Contacts

The Contacts app on your Infinix Note 40 Pro/Pro+ is your central hub for storing and managing contact information for the people you communicate with frequently.

Adding a New Contact:

1. Launch the Contacts App: Locate and tap on the Contacts app icon on your home screen or app drawer. This app is usually represented by a contacts icon or the word "Contacts".
2. Initiate New Contact Creation:
    - Add Button: Look for a "New Contact" or "Add" button (usually a plus sign (+) icon) within the Contacts app. Tapping this button will initiate the process of creating a new contact.
    - From Speed Dial (Possible): Some Infinix models might allow you to create a new contact from the speed dial screen by tapping on an empty slot and selecting "Add contact".
3. Entering Contact Information:
    - Name: Enter the contact's name in the designated field. You can usually add a first name, middle name, and last name.
    - Phone Number: Add the contact's phone number in the designated field. You can typically save multiple

phone numbers for a single contact (e.g., mobile, work, home).
- Additional Information (Optional): Many Contacts apps allow you to add additional information for your contacts such as email addresses, mailing addresses, birthdays, and even custom notes.
4. Saving the Contact:
- Save Button: Once you've entered the desired contact information, tap on the "Save" button (usually located at the bottom of the screen) to save the new contact to your contact list.

Editing Existing Contacts:

1. Open the Contact: Locate and tap on the desired contact you want to edit from your Contacts list. This will open the contact's information page.
2. Editing Information:
   - Tap on any editable field (e.g., name, phone number, email) to modify the information.
   - You can also add additional information fields (e.g., email address, birthday) if they weren't previously included.
3. Saving Changes:
   - Automatic Saving (Possible): After making your edits, some Contacts apps might automatically save the changes.
   - Save Button or Confirmation: Look for a "Save" button or confirmation message if your device requires manual saving.

Additional Contact Management Features (Possible):

- Groups: Some Contacts apps allow you to create groups (e.g., Family, Work, Friends) to organize your contacts.
- Starred Contacts: You can typically "star" important contacts for quick access.
- Sharing Contacts: Some Contacts apps allow you to share contacts with other people through various methods like email or messaging.
- Importing and Exporting Contacts (Possible): Some Contacts apps allow you to import contacts from other devices or storage locations and export your contacts for backup purposes.

By understanding how to add and edit contacts on your Infinix Note 40 Pro/Pro+, you can keep your contact list organized, up-to-date, and ensure you have the latest information for the people you interact with most.

5.2 Creating Groups

Managing a long list of contacts can be cumbersome. Thankfully, the Contacts app on your Infinix Note 40 Pro/Pro+ allows you to create groups to organize your contacts effectively. Assigning contacts to groups like "Family," "Work," or "Close Friends" can streamline your communication and make it easier to find the people you interact with most frequently.

Creating a New Contact Group:

1. Launch the Contacts App: Locate and tap on the Contacts app icon on your home screen or app drawer.

2. Access the Groups Feature (Possible):
   - Groups Tab (Possible): Some Contacts apps have a dedicated "Groups" tab. Tap on the "Groups" tab to access group management features.
   - Menu Button (Possible): If your Contacts app doesn't have a dedicated Groups tab, there might be a menu button (usually three dots (...) or a menu icon). Tap on the menu button and explore options for "Groups" or "Create group".
3. Create New Group:
   - Once you've accessed the Groups section of your Contacts app, look for a "New Group" or "Create group" option. Tapping on this option will initiate the process of creating a new group.
4. Naming Your Group: Enter a name for your new group that clearly identifies its purpose (e.g., "Family," "Work Colleagues," "Gym Buddies").
5. Adding Contacts to the Group (Possible):
   - During Group Creation: Some Contacts apps might allow you to add contacts to the group during the creation process. You might see a list of your contacts where you can select the ones you want to add to the new group.
   - Adding After Creation (Possible): If you weren't able to add contacts during group creation, some Contacts apps allow you to add members after the group is created. Explore the group options (usually by tapping on the group name) to find an "Add member" or "Add contacts" option. You can then select the contacts you want to add to the group from your contact list.

Editing and Managing Groups (Possible):

- Renaming Groups: Some Contacts apps allow you to rename groups by tapping on the group name and selecting an "Edit" or "Rename" option.
- Deleting Groups: Some Contacts apps allow you to delete groups. Be sure to back up your contacts before deleting a group, as removing the group might also remove members' contact information from that group. Explore the group options (usually by tapping on the group name) to find a "Delete" or "Remove group" option.

Using Contact Groups:

- Sending Messages: Some messaging apps allow you to select a group when composing a new message, enabling you to easily send a message to everyone in the group.
- Quick Identification: Having contacts categorized in groups can help you quickly identify individuals within your contact list.

By creating and using groups in your Contacts app, you can organize your contacts efficiently and streamline your communication on your Infinix Note 40 Pro/Pro+.

5.3 Searching for Contacts

Using the Search Bar:

1. Launch the Contacts App: Locate and tap on the Contacts app icon on your home screen or app drawer.

2. Locate the Search Bar: Most Contacts apps have a search bar prominently placed at the top of the screen.
3. Enter Search Keywords: Begin typing the name or any other relevant information about the contact you're searching for. This information could include:
    - Name: Partial or full name of the contact
    - Phone number: Numbers associated with the contact (or a part of the number)
    - Email address: Email addresses associated with the contact (or a part of the email address)
4. Search Results: As you type, the Contacts app will automatically filter and display contacts that match your search criteria. The more specific your search terms, the easier it will be to find the exact contact you need.

Search Tips:

- Case Sensitivity (Possible): Depending on your Contacts app, the search function might be case-sensitive. Experiment with capitalization to improve your search accuracy if needed.
- Contact Information Variations: If you're unsure of the exact spelling of a name or email address, try entering variations to broaden your search results.

Additional Search Features (Possible):

- Contact Groups: Some Contacts apps allow you to filter your search by groups (e.g., "Family," "Work") if your contact is categorized within a group.

5.4 Syncing Contacts

Understanding Syncing:

- Syncing refers to the process of automatically updating information across different devices or platforms.
- When you sync your contacts, any changes you make on one device (e.g., adding a new contact, editing a phone number) will be reflected on your other synced devices.

Syncing with a Google Account:

1. Ensure Google Account Backup is Enabled:
    - Settings: Access your Infinix Note 40 Pro/Pro+ settings. The Settings icon is usually found in the app drawer or by swiping down from the notification bar and tapping on the settings cog.
    - Google Account: Locate the "Accounts" or "Google" section within your settings. Depending on your Android version, the specific wording might differ.
    - Backup and Sync: Tap on your Google Account and ensure "Contacts" is enabled under "Backup & sync" or a similar menu. This ensures your contacts are backed up to your Google Account.
2. Enabling Automatic Syncing:
    - Back to Settings: Navigate back to your phone's main Settings menu.
    - Accounts (Possible): Tap on "Accounts" or "Users & accounts" (depending on your device model).
    - Google Account: Select your Google Account from the list.

- Account Sync (Possible): Ensure "Contacts" is enabled under "Account sync" or a similar menu. This allows your device to automatically sync your contacts with your Google Account.

Benefits of Syncing with Google Account:

- Accessibility: Access your contacts from any device where you're signed in to your Google Account. This could include your phone, computer, or tablet.
- Up-to-Date Information: Changes you make on one device will be reflected on your other synced devices.

Additional Syncing Options (Possible):

- Social Media Syncing: Some social media platforms allow you to sync your contacts with their services. This might involve granting access to your contacts during social media app setup. Be mindful of what information you share with third-party apps.
- Manufacturer Syncing: Some phone manufacturers offer their own cloud syncing services for contacts. Explore your Infinix device's settings to see if this option is available.

Part 3: Unleashing Your Camera

Chapter 6: Capturing Photos and Videos

6.1 Taking Photos in Auto Mode

Open the Camera App:

- Locate and tap on the Camera app icon on your home screen or app drawer. This icon usually resembles a camera lens.

Switching to Auto Mode (if not already in Auto mode):

- Look for a camera mode selection option on your Camera app screen. This might be indicated by icons, text, or a swipe gesture (usually swiping left or right).
- Select "Auto" mode from the available camera mode options. "Auto" mode is typically represented by an icon that resembles a camera or a scene.

Composing Your Shot:

- Use your viewfinder (the large rectangle on your screen) to frame your shot. The viewfinder displays the scene you're pointing the camera at.
- Drag your finger on the screen to move the viewfinder around if your camera has a movable rear camera.

Focusing the Camera:

- Most cameras autofocus automatically. Simply tap on the area of the viewfinder where you want the camera to focus. A focus box or square might appear on your screen to indicate the focused area.

Capturing the Photo:

- Once you've composed your shot and focused the camera, tap on the shutter button (usually a large circle button) on your screen to capture the photo.

Viewing Your Captured Photo:

- The captured photo might be briefly displayed on your screen after taking the picture. You can usually swipe left or right to view previous photos or tap on a thumbnail preview (if available) to view the photo in your gallery app.

Additional Auto Mode Tips:

- Lighting: Auto mode works best in well-lit environments. If lighting is poor, your photos might appear blurry or grainy.
- Stability: Hold your phone steady when capturing photos to minimize blur caused by camera shake.
- Multiple Shots: Don't hesitate to take multiple photos, especially if capturing moving subjects or in low-light conditions.

6.2 Using Different Camera Modes (Portrait, Macro, etc.)

Switching Between Camera Modes:

- Launch the Camera app on your Infinix Note 40 Pro/Pro+.
- Locate the camera mode selection option on your Camera app screen. This might be indicated by icons, text, or a swipe gesture (usually swiping left or right).

Common Camera Modes:

- Portrait: Many Infinix phones offer a Portrait mode that utilizes depth effects to blur the background behind your subject, creating a professional-looking bokeh effect. This mode is ideal for capturing portrait photos of people, pets, or objects where you want the subject to stand out.
- Macro: Macro mode allows you to capture extreme close-up shots, revealing details invisible to the naked eye. This mode is perfect for photographing flowers, insects, or tiny objects. When using Macro mode, ensure good lighting and hold your phone very steady, as even slight movements can cause blur at such close distances.
- Night: Night mode helps capture brighter and clearer photos in low-light environments. It achieves this by extending the camera's exposure time, allowing more light to enter the sensor. However, holding your phone steady is crucial in Night mode to prevent blurry photos due to camera shake. Some Night modes might offer additional options like starry night sky photography.

- Beauty: Beauty mode is designed to enhance portrait photos by smoothing blemishes and evening out skin tones. While it can be a quick fix for imperfections, be cautious of overusing it as it can create an unnatural look.
- Pro (Possible): Some Infinix phones might offer a Pro mode that provides manual control over camera settings like ISO, shutter speed, and white balance. This mode is ideal for experienced users who want more creative control over their photos.

Using the Right Mode for the Scenario:

The key to using camera modes effectively is understanding their strengths and purposes. Here's a quick guideline:

- Auto mode: General everyday photos in good lighting.
- Portrait mode: Portraits of people, pets, or objects with background blur.
- Macro mode: Extreme close-up photos of flowers, insects, or tiny objects.
- Night mode: Photos in low-light environments.
- Beauty mode: Portrait photos with touch-ups (use sparingly).
- Pro mode (if available): Manual control for creative photography (for experienced users).

Exploring Additional Modes:

Your Infinix Note 40 Pro/Pro+ might offer additional camera modes beyond the ones mentioned above. Explore the camera mode selection on your device to discover what it has to offer. Some common additional modes include:

- Panorama: Capture expansive landscapes or group photos.
- Sports: Freeze motion for fast-moving subjects like athletes or pets.
- Video: Record video footage.

By understanding and experimenting with different camera modes, you can unlock the full potential of your Infinix Note 40 Pro/Pro+'s camera and capture stunning photos in various scenarios.

6.3 Recording Videos

Switching to Video Mode:

1. Launch the Camera App: Locate and tap on the Camera app icon on your home screen or app drawer.
2. Locate the Video Mode Option: Look for a video mode selection option on your Camera app screen. This might be indicated by an icon, text label, or a swipe gesture (usually swiping up or down, depending on your device).
3. Switch to Video Mode: Swipe or tap the video mode option to switch the camera app to video recording mode. You'll typically see the viewfinder change aspect ratio to a wider format suitable for videos.

Recording a Video:

1. Compose Your Shot: Frame your shot within the viewfinder, ensuring your subject and area of interest are within the frame.
2. Start Recording: Once you're ready to capture the video, locate the record button (usually a large red circle button)

on your screen. Tap on the record button to begin recording the video.
3. Focusing (Optional): While recording, you can tap on specific areas of the viewfinder to adjust the camera's focus during filming.
4. Zooming (Possible): Some Camera apps allow zooming in and out while recording a video. Look for pinch-to-zoom gestures or on-screen zoom controls (if available) to adjust the zoom level.
5. Stopping Recording: Tap on the record button again (which might turn into a square stop button) to stop recording the video.

Viewing Your Recorded Video:

- After stopping recording, the captured video might be displayed briefly on your screen. You can usually swipe left or right to view previous recordings or tap on a thumbnail preview (if available) to view the video in your gallery app.

Additional Video Recording Tips:

- Orientation: Pay attention to how you hold your phone while recording. Holding it vertically results in portrait-oriented videos, while holding it horizontally captures landscape-oriented videos.
- Stability: Holding your phone steady is crucial for capturing smooth, high-quality videos. Consider using a tripod or mobile gimbal for extra stability, especially when recording long videos or using zoom features.
- Lighting: Just like with photos, good lighting is essential for quality videos. If possible, record in well-lit environments to avoid grainy or blurry footage.

- Audio: The built-in microphone on your phone will record ambient sounds along with the video. Be mindful of background noise and consider using an external microphone for enhanced audio quality in noisy environments (if supported by your device).

6.4 Using Flash, Zoom, and HDR

In this section, we'll explore how to use Flash, Zoom, and HDR to elevate your mobile photography experience.

Using Flash:

- Flash Modes: Most Infinix phones provide multiple flash modes, including:
    - Auto: The camera automatically determines whether to use flash based on lighting conditions.
    - On: The flash fires every time you capture a photo.
    - Off: The flash will not fire, even in low-light conditions.
- Accessing Flash Modes: The location of the flash mode option might vary depending on your Infinix model. It's usually indicated by a lightning bolt icon on your Camera app screen. Tap on the icon to cycle through the available flash modes.
- When to Use Flash: Auto mode is a good option for most situations. Use the "On" mode in low-light environments when you need extra illumination for your photos. Be mindful that using flash directly on subjects can sometimes cause harsh lighting or washed-out colors.

Using Zoom:

- Digital Zoom: Most Infinix phones offer digital zoom functionality. This allows you to magnify your subject but it's important to understand that digital zoom reduces photo quality. The more you zoom in, the more pixelation and loss of detail will occur in your photos.

- Pinching In and Out: You can typically zoom in and out using a pinch-to-zoom gesture on your screen or by using on-screen zoom controls (if available) offered by the Camera app.
- Optical Zoom (Possible): Some Infinix models might have cameras with built-in optical zoom. Optical zoom uses physical lenses to magnify the image, preserving image quality compared to digital zoom. Refer to your Infinix Note 40 Pro/Pro+ user manual or specifications to see if it offers optical zoom capabilities.

Using HDR (High Dynamic Range):

- HDR Technology: HDR stands for High Dynamic Range. When enabled, the Camera app captures multiple exposures of a scene and combines them into a single photo with better dynamic range. This results in a photo with more detail in both the highlights (bright areas) and shadows (dark areas) of the image.
- Enabling HDR: The HDR option might be located within your Camera app settings or shooting mode selection. Look for an HDR icon or setting and enable it when you want to capture scenes with high contrast between light and dark areas.
- When to Use HDR: HDR is beneficial for capturing landscapes, portraits with backlit subjects, or scenes with a mix of bright and dark elements.

Additional Tips:

- Experiment with Flash Modes: Try different flash modes to see how they affect your photos in various lighting conditions.
- Use Zoom Sparingly: While zoom can be helpful for getting closer to subjects, remember that digital zoom reduces quality. If possible, try to move closer to your subject for better results.
- Auto HDR in Challenging Lighting: If you frequently encounter high-contrast scenes, consider enabling Auto HDR in your Camera app settings to automatically capture HDR photos when needed.

Chapter 7: Exploring Advanced Camera Features

7.1 Pro Mode for Manual Controls

Pro Mode for Creative Control:

For photography enthusiasts, Pro mode on your Infinix Note 40 Pro/Pro+ (if available) offers the ability to manually adjust various camera settings, unlocking a higher level of creative control over your photos. Here's a breakdown of some common manual controls you might find in Pro mode:

- ISO: ISO controls the camera's sensitivity to light. A lower ISO is suitable for bright environments, while a higher ISO allows more light into the sensor in low-light conditions (but can also introduce grain).
- Shutter Speed: Shutter speed controls the duration of time the camera sensor is exposed to light. A faster shutter speed freezes motion, while a slower shutter speed allows more light in but can cause blur in moving subjects or with camera shake.
- Exposure: Exposure refers to the overall brightness of your photo. It's determined by the combination of ISO and shutter speed settings.
- White Balance: White balance adjusts the color temperature of your photo to match the lighting conditions (e.g., incandescent, fluorescent, daylight).
- Focus: Pro mode might allow manual focus, letting you choose the specific area you want the camera to focus on.

Using Pro Mode Effectively:

- Understanding Exposure Triangle: The relationship between ISO, shutter speed, and aperture (controlled indirectly through exposure compensation in Pro mode) is known as the exposure triangle. Adjusting one setting affects the others, so it's crucial to understand their interplay to achieve your desired results.
- Experimentation is Key: Pro mode offers a wide range of possibilities. Don't be afraid to experiment with different settings to see how they affect your photos. Start by taking multiple photos with slight adjustments to understand the impact of each setting.
- Learning Resources: There are many online resources and tutorials available that delve deeper into manual photography concepts and using Pro mode effectively.

Benefits of Pro Mode:

- Creative Control: Pro mode empowers you to achieve specific visual effects and artistic styles that automatic modes might not capture.
- Low-Light Photography: By adjusting ISO and shutter speed, you can capture better photos in low-light environments compared to relying solely on auto mode.
- Depth-of-Field Control (Possible): Some Pro modes might offer manual aperture control (indirectly through exposure compensation), allowing you to control the depth of field and create bokeh effects (blurred backgrounds).

Pro Mode Challenges:

- Learning Curve: Mastering manual controls takes practice and understanding of photography principles.
- Not for Everyone: Pro mode might be overwhelming for casual users who prefer point-and-shoot simplicity.
- Potential for Poor Results: Using Pro mode without understanding the settings can lead to blurry, grainy, or over/underexposed photos.

Pro mode on your Infinix Note 40 Pro/Pro+ opens doors to creative photography possibilities.

7.2 Using the Macro Lens (if applicable)

Magnifying the Miniature World:

The macro lens on your Infinix Note 40 Pro/Pro+ (if equipped) allows you to capture close-up photos of tiny objects, revealing details invisible to the naked eye. This is perfect for photographing nature's wonders like insects, flowers, dewdrops, or intricate textures on objects like coins or jewelry.

Switching to Macro Mode:

- Macro Mode Selection: The way to access Macro mode might vary depending on your Infinix model. Here are some common possibilities:
    - Dedicated Macro Mode: Look for a "Macro" mode option within your camera mode selection menu.

- Flower/Plant Icon (Possible): Some Infinix camera apps might use a flower or plant icon to represent Macro mode.
- Super Close-Up Option (Possible): The Macro mode might be labeled as "Super close-up" or similar wording within the camera app.

Capturing Macro Photos:

1. Ensure Macro Mode is On: Switch to the Macro mode using the method mentioned above.
2. Get Close to Your Subject: The macro lens requires you to get very close to your subject, typically much closer than you would for regular photos. Refer to your camera app's instructions or on-screen guide (if available) for the ideal macro lens shooting distance.
3. Focus and Stability: Macro photos require precise focus due to the close distance. Tap on the area of your viewfinder where you want the camera to focus. Holding your phone very steady is crucial to avoid blurry photos at such high magnification. You might even consider using a tripod for extra stability.
4. Lighting: Good lighting is essential for capturing sharp macro photos. If possible, use natural light for the best results. Avoid using flash directly on your macro subject, as it can create harsh glare.

Macro Photography Tips:

- Experiment with Angles: Don't be afraid to experiment with different shooting angles to find the most compelling composition for your macro photos.

- Background Consideration: Pay attention to the background in your macro shots. A clean background can make your subject stand out.
- Highlight Details: Macro lenses allow you to capture intricate details. Use this to your advantage to showcase the unique textures or patterns of your subject.

7.3 Slow-Motion Recording

Slowing Down Time:

Slow-Motion recording allows you to capture videos at a higher frame rate than the standard playback rate. When played back at a normal speed, this creates a slow-motion effect, making fast-moving actions appear to be stretched out in time.

This technique can be used to add drama, suspense, or a unique visual aesthetic to your videos.

Activating Slow-Motion Mode:

- Launch the Camera App: Locate and tap on the Camera app icon on your home screen or app drawer.
- Access Recording Modes: Swipe or tap through the recording mode options (usually swiping left or right) to find Slow-Motion mode. It might be signified by an icon or text label.

Recording in Slow-Motion:

1. Choose Slow-Motion Speed (Possible): Some Infinix camera apps might allow you to choose from different slow-motion recording speeds. Select the desired speed before starting your recording. Slower speeds will create a more dramatic slow-motion effect but will also shorten the total recorded duration in slow-motion.
2. Compose Your Shot: Frame your shot within the viewfinder, ensuring the action you want to capture in slow-motion is within the frame.
3. Start Recording: Tap on the record button to begin recording in slow-motion mode.
4. Capture the Action: Focus on capturing the fast-moving moment you want to slow down. Remember, the recorded slow-motion footage will be shorter than the real-time action.
5. Stop Recording: Tap on the record button again to stop recording.

Playing Back Your Slow-Motion Video:

- After recording, your video might be displayed briefly on the screen. You can typically swipe left or right to view previous recordings or tap on a thumbnail preview (if available) to view the video in your gallery app.
- When played back in your gallery app, the video will be played back in slow-motion at the speed you selected during recording.

Slow-Motion Recording Tips:

- Predictable Actions: Slow-motion works best for capturing predictable actions that unfold over a short period, such as a splash of water, a jump, or a quick burst of movement.

- Good Lighting: Adequate lighting is essential for good slow-motion footage.
- Short Bursts: It's best to record short bursts in slow-motion mode due to the limited recording duration at slower speeds. You can then edit these clips together later in your preferred video editing app.
- Editing (Optional): You can use video editing software on your phone or computer to further enhance your slow-motion clips by trimming unwanted footage or adding music and effects.

By understanding how to use Slow-Motion recording (if available) on your Infinix Note 40 Pro/Pro+, you can add a creative touch to your videos and capture fleeting moments in a dramatic and visually captivating way. So experiment, have fun, and slow down the world around you with your phone's camera!

7.4 AI photography Made Easy: Enhance Your Photos with Intelligence

AI Camera Features Disclaimer:

The world of smartphone cameras is constantly evolving, and AI (Artificial Intelligence) is playing an increasingly important role.

While many Infinix phones are incorporating AI features, the specific functionalities might vary depending on the model and software version. Consult your Infinix Note 40 Pro/Pro+ user manual or explore your Camera app settings to see if it offers AI-powered features.

The Power of AI in Photography:

AI is transforming smartphone photography by automating tasks and offering intelligent assistance to capture better photos. Here are some common AI features you might find on your Infinix Note 40 Pro/Pro+ (if applicable):

- Scene Detection: The camera app might use AI to automatically detect the scene you're pointing the camera at (e.g., portrait, landscape, night). It can then adjust camera settings like exposure, white balance, and color saturation for an optimal photo in that particular scenario.
- Object Recognition: AI can recognize objects within the frame and optimize settings to capture them clearly. For example, it might adjust focus and exposure for faces in portrait mode or enhance colors in a flower shot.
- AI Beauty Mode (Possible): Some Infinix phones might offer an AI-powered Beauty mode that uses facial recognition to apply subtle enhancements while preserving natural-looking results.
- Shot Suggestions (Possible): AI might analyze the scene and suggest optimal compositions or shooting angles to help you frame your photos more effectively.

Benefits of AI Photography:

- Effortless Enhancement: AI features can simplify capturing good photos, especially for casual users who might not be familiar with manual camera settings.
- Improved Results: AI can analyze the scene and adjust settings for better exposure, color balance, and overall image quality.
- Creative Inspiration (Possible): AI-powered shot suggestions can help you explore different compositions and capture unique perspectives.

Using AI Camera Features:

- Identify AI Modes: Explore your Camera app settings or shooting mode options to find AI-powered features. They might be signified by specific icons or labels like "AI," "Scene detection," or "AI Mode."
- Enable AI Features: Turn on the AI features you want to use within the Camera app settings.
- Compose and Shoot: Frame your shot as usual. The AI will analyze the scene and automatically adjust settings for optimal results.

Important Considerations:

- Not a Replacement for Knowledge: While AI can simplify photography, understanding basic photographic principles can still be helpful for capturing even better photos.
- Overly Artificial Results (Possible): Be mindful of the level of AI enhancement, especially in beauty mode, to avoid overly processed or unnatural-looking photos.

AI camera features on your Infinix Note 40 Pro/Pro+ (if applicable) can be a valuable tool to enhance your mobile photography experience. By understanding these features and using them effectively, you can capture stunning photos effortlessly and unleash your creativity with minimal technical know-how. Remember, AI is there to assist you, and experimenting alongside these features can further improve your photography skills!

Chapter 8: Camera Settings and Customization

8.1 Adjusting Photo and Video Resolution

The resolution of your photos and videos determines the amount of detail captured and the overall file size. Higher resolution photos and videos will contain more detail but will also take up more storage space on your device. Here's a guide on adjusting photo and video resolution on your Infinix Note 40 Pro/Pro+

Understanding Resolution:

- Photo Resolution: Photo resolution is typically measured in megapixels (MP). Higher megapixel count signifies more detail and a larger image size. For example, a 12MP photo captures more detail than a 5MP photo.
- Video Resolution: Video resolution is usually denoted by width x height pixels and frame rate (fps). Common video resolutions include 1080p (1920 x 1080 pixels) and 4K (3840 x 2160 pixels). Higher resolutions offer sharper videos but come with larger file sizes.

Adjusting Photo Resolution:

1. Launch the Camera App: Locate and tap on the Camera app icon on your home screen or app drawer.
2. Access Settings: Look for the Settings icon within the Camera app. It might be represented by a gear icon or by

swiping down on the screen (depending on your device model).
- Settings Location Variation: The location of the settings menu might vary slightly depending on your Infinix model. Explore your Camera app to find the settings option.
1. Photo Resolution Options: Within the Camera app settings, navigate to the section related to photo size or resolution. You might see options for different megapixel resolutions (e.g., 12MP, 8MP, 5MP).
2. Choosing a Photo Resolution: Select the desired photo resolution based on your needs. Consider the following:
    - Storage Space: Higher megapixel photos take up more storage space. Choose a lower resolution if you're running low on storage or if you don't need to print your photos at large sizes.
    - Print Size: If you plan to print your photos, choose a higher resolution to ensure enough detail for good quality prints.
    - Sharing: For sharing photos online or on social media, a lower resolution might be sufficient.

Adjusting Video Resolution:

1. Access Camera Settings (Refer to Steps 1 & 2 from Photo Resolution Adjustments): Launch the Camera app and locate the Camera app settings menu.
2. Video Resolution Options: Navigate to the section related to video resolution or video recording size within the Camera app settings. You might see options for different video resolutions (e.g., 1080p, 720p, 4K) and frame rates (fps).

3. **Choosing a Video Resolution:** Select the desired video resolution based on your needs. Consider the following:
    - Storage Space: Higher resolution videos (like 4K) take up significantly more storage space than lower resolutions (like 720p).
    - Video Sharing: If you plan to share your videos online or on social media, a lower resolution might be sufficient for uploading and playback.
    - Video Editing (Optional): If you plan to edit your videos extensively, choosing a higher resolution can provide more detail for cropping or zooming during editing.
    - Display Quality: Consider the resolution of the screen you'll be viewing the video on. A 4K video won't be visually superior if you're only watching it on a standard definition (SD) screen.

Additional Tips:

- Experiment with Different Resolutions: Try capturing photos and videos at different resolutions to see how they affect image/video quality and file size on your device.
- Auto Mode (Possible): Some Camera apps offer an "Auto" mode that might adjust resolution based on available storage space or other factors.
- Check Storage Space: Keep an eye on your device's storage and adjust photo/video resolution accordingly if you're running low on space.

8.2 Customizing Image Quality

Understanding Image Quality:

Image quality refers to the overall clarity, detail, and color accuracy of a photo. Several factors contribute to image quality, including:

- Resolution: Higher resolution captures more detail, but also creates larger file sizes.
- Compression: Compressed images are smaller in size but may lose some detail compared to uncompressed images.
- Color Depth: Color depth determines the number of bits used to represent color information in a photo. Higher color depth translates to richer and more accurate colors.
- File Format: Common image file formats like JPEG use compression, while formats like PNG offer lossless compression but create larger files.

Customizing Image Quality Settings (Possible):

While not all Infinix models offer extensive image quality customization options within the Camera app, some devices provide more control. Here's what you might find:

- Image Quality/Compression Setting: Look for a setting labeled "Image quality" or "Compression" within your Camera app settings. This might offer options like "Fine," "Normal," or "Low." Higher quality settings will result in larger file sizes with more detail preserved.

- JPEG Quality Adjustment (Possible): Some Infinix camera apps might allow you to adjust the JPEG quality level directly. A slider or numerical scale will let you choose between higher quality (larger files) and lower quality (smaller files).

Balancing Image Quality and File Size:

The ideal image quality settings depend on your priorities. Here's a breakdown to help you decide:

- Prioritize Image Quality: Choose higher quality or lower compression settings if you need maximum detail and plan to print your photos or edit them extensively. Be aware that this will result in larger file sizes.
- Focus on Storage Space: If you're low on storage space or plan to share photos online where some detail loss might be acceptable, choose lower quality or higher compression settings for smaller file sizes.

Additional Tips:

- Experiment with Settings: Try capturing photos at different quality settings to see how they affect image quality and file size on your device.
- Default Settings: The default camera settings on your Infinix Note 40 Pro/Pro+ are likely chosen for a good balance between image quality and file size. You can adjust them based on your needs.
- External Storage (Optional): Consider using a microSD card if you plan to capture many high-quality photos and need more storage space on your device.

8.3 White Balance and Exposure Controls

White Balance:

- Color Accuracy: White balance refers to the camera's ability to reproduce colors accurately under different lighting conditions. Proper white balance ensures that whites appear white, and other colors are portrayed realistically.
- Lighting Variations: Natural light (daylight) has a specific color temperature. Artificial lighting sources like incandescent bulbs or fluorescent lights have different color temperatures that can affect how colors appear in your photos.
- White Balance Modes: Most Infinix camera apps offer various white balance modes to adjust for different lighting conditions. Here are some common options:
    - Auto White Balance (AWB): The default setting, AWB attempts to automatically adjust the white balance based on the lighting scene. It works well under many conditions but might not be perfect in all situations.

- Incandescent: Use this mode for photos taken under incandescent lighting (yellowish hue) to achieve a more natural look.
- Fluorescent: Use this mode for photos taken under fluorescent lighting (often greenish or bluish tint) to produce more natural color reproduction.
- Daylight: Use this mode for outdoor photos taken under natural daylight conditions for optimal color accuracy.
- Cloudy: Use this mode for photos taken on cloudy days when the sunlight appears cooler or bluish.

Setting White Balance:

- Accessing White Balance: The location of the white balance settings might vary slightly depending on your Infinix model. It's usually found within the Camera app settings or shooting mode options. Look for an icon or setting labeled "White Balance" or "WB."
- Choosing the Right Mode: Select the white balance mode that best reflects the lighting conditions under which you're capturing your photo. If you're unsure, experiment with different modes to see which one produces the most natural-looking colors in your photos.

Exposure:

- Balancing Light: Exposure refers to the total amount of light that reaches the camera sensor during a photo. Balanced exposure creates photos that are neither too bright (overexposed) nor too dark (underexposed).
- Exposure Compensation: Most Camera apps offer Exposure compensation, a tool that allows you to adjust the

camera's automatic exposure settings. This is useful when the auto settings might not produce the desired brightness in your photos.
- Adjusting Exposure: Exposure compensation is typically represented by a +/- scale. A positive value (+) increases exposure, making the photo brighter. Conversely, a negative value (-) decreases exposure, making the photo darker.
- Using Exposure Compensation: Here's a general guideline for using exposure compensation:
  - Overexposed Photos: If your photos appear too bright with washed-out colors, use a negative exposure compensation value to darken the image.
  - Underexposed Photos: If your photos appear too dark and lack detail, use a positive exposure compensation value to brighten the image.

Taking Control with Manual Mode (Possible):

- Advanced Control (Possible): If your Infinix Note 40 Pro/Pro+ offers a Pro mode in the Camera app, you might have even more control over white balance and exposure. Pro mode might allow you to manually set the white balance temperature (in kelvins) and adjust shutter speed and ISO, which directly affect exposure.

By understanding white balance and exposure, and using the settings available on your Infinix Note 40 Pro/Pro+ (including automatic and manual controls if applicable), you can capture photos with accurate colors and proper brightness in various lighting conditions. Mastering these concepts will elevate your mobile photography skills and help you achieve professional-looking results!

Part 4: Maximizing Functionality

Chapter 9: Fingerprint Unlock and Facial Recognition

Your Infinix Note 40 Pro/Pro+ likely offers two common biometric security options: Fingerprint Unlock and Facial Recognition.

Fingerprint Unlock:

Fingerprint Unlock utilizes your fingerprint as a unique identifier to unlock your Infinix Note 40 Pro/Pro+. Here's a general guide on setting it up:

Prerequisites:

- Clean and dry fingers.
- A spare moment to complete the setup process without interruptions.

Setting Up Fingerprint Unlock:

1. Access Security Settings: Locate and tap on the Settings app on your home screen. Then, navigate to the Security or Security & Privacy section depending on your device model.
2. Find Fingerprint Unlock: Within the security settings, look for a section or setting labeled Fingerprint Unlock, Fingerprint ID, or similar wording.

3. **Enroll Your Fingerprint:** Tap on the fingerprint option and follow the on-screen prompts to enroll your fingerprint. You will likely be required to place your finger on the fingerprint sensor (usually located on the back of the phone or under the display) multiple times to capture different angles of your fingerprint.
4. **Set Up Backup PIN (Recommended):** It's highly recommended to create a backup PIN or password in case the fingerprint sensor malfunctions or you're unable to use your fingerprint to unlock your phone.

Using Fingerprint Unlock:

1. **Wake Up Your Phone:** Press the power button or tap the screen to wake up your device.
2. **Place Finger on Sensor:** When the lock screen appears, place your enrolled finger on the fingerprint sensor.
3. **Access Granted (If Successful):** If the fingerprint sensor recognizes your fingerprint, your phone will be unlocked.

Facial Recognition:

Facial Recognition utilizes your face as a biometric identifier to unlock your Infinix Note 40 Pro/Pro+. Here's a general guide on setting it up:

Prerequisites:

- Good lighting conditions.
- Remove any hats, scarves, glasses, or masks that might obscure your facial features during the setup process.

Setting Up Facial Recognition:

1. Access Security Settings: Locate and tap on the Settings app on your home screen. Then, navigate to the Security or Security & Privacy section depending on your device model.
2. Find Facial Recognition: Within the security settings, look for a section or setting labeled Facial Recognition, Face Unlock, or similar wording.
3. Enroll Your Face: Tap on the facial recognition option and follow the on-screen prompts to enroll your face. You will likely need to position your face within the phone's frame and move your head slowly as instructed to capture your facial features from different angles.
4. Set Up Backup PIN (Recommended): It's highly recommended to create a backup PIN or password in case the facial recognition system malfunctions or you're unable to unlock your phone with your face.

Using Facial Recognition:

1. Wake Up Your Phone: Press the power button or tap the screen to wake up your device.
2. Look at Your Phone: When the lock screen appears, glance at your phone ensuring your face is within the view of the front-facing camera.
3. Access Granted (If Successful): If the facial recognition system recognizes your face, your phone will be unlocked.

Additional Tips:

- Fingerprint Sensor Placement: When enrolling your fingerprint, ensure you're comfortably placing your finger on the sensor in a way you'll naturally use to unlock your phone.

- Multiple Fingerprints (Possible): Some Infinix phones allow enrolling multiple fingerprints for added convenience and security.
- Lighting Conditions: Facial recognition might work less effectively in low-light conditions. Consider setting up fingerprint unlock as a backup for such scenarios.
- Security Considerations: Both fingerprint unlock and facial recognition offer a level of convenience but might not be entirely secure compared to strong passwords or PINs. Consider your security needs when choosing your preferred unlock method.

Chapter 10: Connecting to Wi-Fi and Sharing Your Connection

10.1 Connecting to Wi-Fi Networks

Requirements:

- The name (SSID) and password of the Wi-Fi network you want to connect to.

Connecting to a Wi-Fi Network:

1. Open the Settings App: Locate and tap on the Settings app icon on your home screen, usually represented by a gear or cog symbol.
2. Access Wi-Fi Settings: Navigate to the Wi-Fi section within the Settings app. On some Infinix models, you might swipe down on the notification panel and tap the Wi-Fi icon to access the settings directly.
3. Turn on Wi-Fi (if not already on): Toggle the Wi-Fi switch ON. You will see a list of available Wi-Fi networks within the range of your device.
4. Choose the Network: Select the Wi-Fi network you want to connect to from the list.
5. Enter Password (if required): If the network is password-protected, a pop-up will appear prompting you to enter the Wi-Fi password. Enter the correct password for the chosen network and tap Connect.

6. Connection Status: Your device will try to connect to the Wi-Fi network. You might see a connection status message while it establishes the connection.

Congratulations! Once the connection is successful, you will see the Wi-Fi network name connected with a signal strength indicator next to it in your Wi-Fi settings or notification bar. You can now access the internet through the connected Wi-Fi network.

Connecting to a Hidden Network (Possible):

Some Wi-Fi networks might be hidden. If you need to connect to a hidden network, follow these additional steps:

1. Tap on "Add network" (or similar wording) at the bottom of the available networks list in the Wi-Fi settings.
2. Enter the Network Name (SSID) of the hidden Wi-Fi network.
3. Select the Security type (usually WPA2 PSK for home Wi-Fi networks).
4. Enter the Wi-Fi password for the hidden network.
5. Tap "Save" or "Connect" to attempt connecting to the hidden network.

Additional Tips:

- If you connect to a private network, you might be prompted to accept the network's security certificate. Tap "Accept" or "Trust" to proceed.
- Forget Wi-Fi networks you no longer use by tapping and holding on the network name in the Wi-Fi settings list and selecting "Forget" or "Remove".

- You can set your preferred Wi-Fi network as the default network so your device connects to it automatically when in range. Tap and hold on the preferred network name and select "Set as default network" (if available).

10.2 Creating a Mobile Hotspot

Before You Start:

- Mobile Data Enabled: Ensure you have mobile data enabled on your Infinix Note 40 Pro/Pro+ and a stable data connection. Mobile hotspot functionality typically utilizes your device's cellular data for internet access.
- Data Plan Consideration: Sharing your internet connection via a mobile hotspot might incur additional charges depending on your mobile data plan. Be sure to check your data plan details to avoid unexpected charges.

Activating Mobile Hotspot:

The steps to activate a mobile hotspot might vary slightly depending on your Infinix model. Here's a general guide:

1. Access Settings: Locate and tap on the Settings app on your home screen. This is usually represented by an icon resembling a gear or cog.
2. Find Mobile Hotspot: Navigate to the section labeled Mobile Hotspot, Wi-Fi Hotspot, Tethering, or similar wording within the Settings app.

3. Turn on Hotspot: Toggle the Mobile Hotspot/Wi-Fi Hotspot switch ON. You might see a pop-up informing you about data usage while hotspot mode is active.
4. Configure Hotspot Details (Optional): Tap on the hotspot name (SSID) or security settings to customize them if desired. You can create a unique name for your hotspot and set a strong password to protect your connection.
5. Connecting Other Devices: On your other device (laptop, tablet, etc.), search for available Wi-Fi networks. You should see the hotspot name you created from your Infinix phone listed among the available networks.
6. Enter Hotspot Password: Select the hotspot network name and enter the password you created (or the default password displayed on your Infinix phone) to connect the other device to your mobile hotspot.

Congratulations! The other device should now be connected to the internet through your Infinix Note 40 Pro/Pro+'s mobile hotspot.

Managing Mobile Hotspot:

- You can access the Mobile Hotspot settings again to monitor data usage while hotspot mode is active or to change the hotspot name or password.
- To turn off the Mobile Hotspot, simply toggle the Mobile Hotspot/Wi-Fi Hotspot switch OFF in the settings.

Additional Tips:

- While connected to your mobile hotspot, data usage on the connected devices will count towards your mobile data plan.

- For better security, it's recommended to use a strong password for your mobile hotspot and avoid connecting unknown devices.
- Consider your data plan limitations when using a mobile hotspot to avoid exceeding your data allowance and incurring extra charges.

Chapter 11: Pairing with Bluetooth Devices

11.1 Connecting to Bluetooth Headphones or Speakers

Requirements:

- Your Bluetooth headphones or speakers must be turned on and discoverable (refer to their user manual if needed). This usually involves pressing a specific button on the device to make it visible for pairing.
- Your Infinix Note 40 Pro/Pro+ has Bluetooth enabled.

Connecting to a Bluetooth Audio Device:

1. Access Settings: Locate and tap on the Settings app on your home screen, usually represented by a gear or cog icon.
2. Find Bluetooth: Navigate to the Bluetooth section within the Settings app.
3. Turn on Bluetooth (if not already on): Toggle the Bluetooth switch ON to activate Bluetooth on your Infinix device.
4. Scan for Devices: Tap on "Scan for devices" or a similar option to initiate a search for Bluetooth devices within range.
5. Select Audio Device: Your Infinix Note 40 Pro/Pro+ will display a list of detected Bluetooth devices. Choose the name of your headphones or speaker from the list.

6. Pairing Request (if needed): You might see a pairing request pop-up on your phone or a PIN confirmation request on your headphones/speaker. Confirm the pairing on both devices to proceed.
7. Connection Successful: Once pairing is complete, your Infinix Note 40 Pro/Pro+ will be connected to your Bluetooth audio device. You should see the connected device name under your Bluetooth settings or in the notification bar.

Playing Audio Through Bluetooth:

- After successful pairing, audio from your Infinix Note 40 Pro/Pro+ (e.g., music, videos, games) will be routed to the connected Bluetooth headphones or speaker.
- You can control music playback (play/pause, volume) using the media controls on your phone or the controls on your Bluetooth audio device (if available).

Disconnecting or Changing Bluetooth Devices:

- To disconnect a Bluetooth audio device, tap on the connected device name under the Bluetooth settings and select "Disconnect" or "Forget".
- You can connect to other Bluetooth audio devices by repeating the pairing steps mentioned earlier. Your Infinix Note 40 Pro/Pro+ can remember multiple Bluetooth devices and allow you to switch between them easily.

Additional Tips:

- Bluetooth connection range might vary depending on the devices. Ensure your phone and Bluetooth audio device are within a reasonable range for optimal connectivity.
- Some Bluetooth headphones or speakers might require manual selection of audio output on the device itself after connecting via Bluetooth. Refer to the user manual of your Bluetooth audio device if you face any difficulties.
- For better sound quality during calls, ensure your Infinix Note 40 Pro/Pro+ is connected to a Bluetooth headset that supports the aptX or similar high-quality audio codecs (if applicable).

11.2 Transferring Files via Bluetooth

Before You Begin:

- Bluetooth Enabled on Both Devices: Ensure Bluetooth is turned on and functioning on both your Infinix Note 40 Pro/Pro+ and the device you want to transfer files to/from (another phone, laptop, etc.).
- Visibility and Pairing: The receiving device might need to be set to discoverable (visible to other Bluetooth devices). If the devices haven't been paired before, you'll need to complete the pairing process before initiating a file transfer. (Refer to the previous guide on Connecting to Bluetooth Headphones or Speakers for pairing instructions if needed)

Transferring Files from Your Infinix Note 40 Pro/Pro+ (if applicable):

1. Locate the File You Want to Transfer: Open the File Manager app or the app where your desired file is located (e.g., Photos app for images).
2. Select the File: Browse and tap to select the file you want to transfer via Bluetooth.
3. Share Menu: Once the file is selected, tap the Share button or similar menu option (depending on the app). This will typically be represented by three dots or an icon with sharing arrows.
4. Select Bluetooth: In the share menu, look for a Bluetooth icon or option labeled "Bluetooth" or "Share via Bluetooth."
5. Choose Receiving Device: Your Infinix Note 40 Pro/Pro+ (if applicable) will scan for discoverable Bluetooth devices in range. Select the name of the device you want to transfer the file to.
6. Confirmation (if needed): On the receiving device, you might be prompted to accept the incoming Bluetooth file transfer. Confirm the transfer to proceed.
7. Transfer Progress: You will see a progress bar on your Infinix Note 40 Pro/Pro+ (if applicable) indicating the file transfer process.

Receiving Files via Bluetooth (if applicable):

1. Make Your Device Discoverable: Ensure your Infinix Note 40 Pro/Pro+ (if applicable) is turned on, Bluetooth is enabled, and the device is set to discoverable (visible to other Bluetooth devices).

2. File Transfer Initiated from Another Device: The other device initiating the transfer will search for Bluetooth devices and send the file.
3. Accepting the Transfer: On your Infinix Note 40 Pro/Pro+ (if applicable), you will receive a notification about an incoming Bluetooth file transfer. Tap "Accept" or "Receive" to confirm and begin receiving the file.
4. Saving the Received File: You might be prompted to choose a location to save the received file on your Infinix device. Select the desired storage location and confirm to save the file.

Important Notes:

- Limited File Size (Possible): Some Infinix models might have limitations on the file size transferable via Bluetooth.
- Slower Transfer Speeds: Bluetooth transfers are generally slower compared to Wi-Fi Direct or cable connections.
- Compatibility: File transfer functionality and limitations might vary depending on the Bluetooth version supported by your Infinix Note 40 Pro/Pro+ (if applicable) and the receiving device.

Alternatives for File Transfer:

If your Infinix Note 40 Pro/Pro+ doesn't support Bluetooth file transfer, consider alternative methods like:

- Wi-Fi Direct: If both devices support Wi-Fi Direct, it can offer faster file transfer speeds than Bluetooth.
- Cloud Storage Services: Upload the files to a cloud storage service (e.g., Google Drive, Dropbox) and access them from the other device.

- Cable Connection (if applicable): If both devices have appropriate ports (e.g., USB), a cable connection can provide the fastest and most reliable file transfer method.

By following these steps (if applicable) and considering the alternatives, you can transfer files between your Infinix Note 40 Pro/Pro+ and other devices using Bluetooth whenever possible. Remember, Bluetooth file transfer functionality might vary depending on your specific device model.

Chapter 12: Optimizing Battery Life

12.1 Understanding Battery Usage

Here's a breakdown of factors that impact battery life and how they affect your device:

Factor	Description	Impact on Battery Life
Display Brightness	The higher the screen brightness, the more battery power it consumes.	Significant
Screen Timeout	The time it takes for the screen to turn off after inactivity.	Moderate
App Activity	Certain apps, especially those with high processing demands, GPS usage, or constant	Varies depending on the app

	background refresh, drain battery faster.	
Background Processes	Unnecessary apps running in the background can consume battery even when not actively used.	Moderate
Cellular Data vs. Wi-Fi	Cellular data usage generally consumes more battery than Wi-Fi connections.	Significant
Bluetooth Connectivity	Maintaining a Bluetooth connection can drain battery, especially for audio streaming or data transfer.	Moderate
Location Services	Enabling location services for apps	Varies depending on usage

	can consume battery power.	
Battery Age	Batteries degrade over time and lose capacity, leading to shorter battery life.	Significant (gradually worsens)
Operating System Version	Newer operating systems may be optimized for better battery efficiency.	Can be positive or negative depending on the update
Signal Strength	Searching for a weak signal can drain battery life faster.	Moderate
Extreme Temperatures	Both very hot and cold temperatures can reduce battery life.	Moderate

12.2 Enabling Battery-Saving Features

Accessing Battery Settings:

1. Locate and tap on the Settings app on your home screen. This is usually represented by an icon resembling a gear or cog.
2. Navigate to the Battery section within the Settings app. On some Infinix models, you might find it under Performance or Device Care.

Understanding Battery Usage:

The Battery settings will typically display information on your battery usage. You'll see details like:

- Overall battery level and estimated remaining time
- Percentage of battery consumption by different apps and system functions

By understanding which apps and features consume the most battery, you can identify areas for improvement.

Activating Battery Saver Mode:

Most Infinix devices come with a built-in Battery Saver mode that reduces power consumption by limiting background activity, restricting app refresh rates, and lowering screen brightness. Here's how to activate it:

1. Within the Battery settings, locate the Battery Saver option.

2. Toggle the Battery Saver switch ON. You might see an option to choose from different Battery Saver modes (if available) offering varying levels of power-saving intensity.

Customizing Battery Saver Settings (if applicable):

Some Infinix models might allow you to customize Battery Saver options. Here are some common settings you might find:

- Schedule Battery Saver: Set Battery Saver to activate automatically at a specific time or when the battery level reaches a certain percentage.
- Exempt Apps (if applicable): Choose specific apps that you want to run normally even in Battery Saver mode (e.g., messaging apps for staying notified).
- Background Activity Restrictions: Control the level of background activity for apps to further optimize battery usage.

Additional Battery-Saving Tips:

- Adjust Screen Brightness: Reduce screen brightness to a comfortable level. This is one of the most significant factors impacting battery life.
- Optimize Location Services: Enable location services only for apps that require them. Disable location access for unused apps to save battery.
- Manage Background Processes: Close any unnecessary apps running in the background that you're not actively using.
- Wi-Fi vs. Cellular Data: Whenever possible, connect to Wi-Fi networks as they consume less battery compared to cellular data.

- Bluetooth Off When Not in Use: Turn off Bluetooth when you're not using any Bluetooth devices (headphones, speakers, etc.) to save battery.
- Auto-Sync and App Refresh: Limit automatic syncing of emails, social media accounts, and other apps to reduce battery drain.
- Software Updates: Install the latest software updates for your Infinix Note 40 Pro/Pro+ as they might include battery efficiency improvements.

12.3 Charging Your Phone

What You'll Need:

- The charger that came with your Infinix Note 40 Pro/Pro+ (or a compatible charger)
- A power outlet

Steps:

1. Plug the Charger into an Outlet: Find a wall outlet and plug the power adapter of your charger into it.
2. Connect the Charging Cable to Your Phone: Take the charging cable (usually USB-A to USB-C) and connect the USB-C end to the charging port on your Infinix Note 40 Pro/Pro+.
3. Charging Notification: Once properly connected, you should see a charging indicator on your phone's screen, typically a lightning bolt symbol or a battery icon filling up.

Optional but Recommended Tips:

- Power Off or Use While Charging: You can use your phone while it's charging, but for slightly faster charging, consider turning it off or keeping it in airplane mode to minimize background activity.
- Avoid Extreme Temperatures: While charging, try to avoid leaving your phone in excessively hot or cold environments as this can negatively impact battery health.
- Using the Correct Charger: It's recommended to use the original charger that came with your Infinix Note 40

Pro/Pro+ or a certified charger compatible with your device. This helps ensure proper charging rates and safety.
- Clean the Charging Port (Occasionally): Dust, debris, or lint accumulated in the charging port can hinder charging efficiency. Occasionally, use a compressed air can (without inserting the nozzle) to gently clean the port.

Additional Notes:

- Fast Charging (if supported): Some Infinix models support fast charging technologies. If your phone and charger support fast charging, you'll see a faster rise in the battery level indicator initially.
- Wireless Charging (if supported): A few Infinix models might also support wireless charging. In that case, you would place your phone on a compatible wireless charging pad (sold separately) to initiate charging.

Part 5: XOS Customization

Chapter 13: Personalizing Your XOS Experience

Visual Customization:

- Themes: XOS often offers a variety of built-in themes or a theme store where you can download and apply themes that change the overall look and feel of your phone's interface, including wallpapers, icons, and accent colors. Explore the theme options and choose one that suits your style.
- Wallpapers & Lock Screens: Set a personal wallpaper for your home screen and lock screen using your favorite photos or images. You can also explore live wallpapers or animated lock screens for a more dynamic look (options might vary depending on your device model).
- Icon Packs: Some Infinix models allow applying icon packs that change the appearance of app icons on your home screen and app drawer. This can further personalize the visual style of your device.

Optimizing Functionality:

- Home Screen Layout: Personalize your home screen by arranging app icons, creating folders for app organization, and adding widgets for quick access to information and frequently used functions.
- Notification Panel: Customize what information appears in your notification panel by managing app notifications and

rearranging quick settings tiles for easy access to Wi-Fi, Bluetooth, flashlight, and other functions.
- Sounds & Vibrations: Set custom ringtones and notification sounds for different apps and contacts. You can also adjust vibration patterns and system sounds to your preference.

XOS Features (Explore Built-in Apps):

- XOS Launcher Settings: The launcher settings contains options like auto-rotate, transition effects, and app drawer style (app drawer appearance).
- Xcare or XOS Security: These built-in apps might offer features like app permissions management, system optimization tools, and security scans to personalize your phone's security and performance.
- Other Pre-installed Apps: Some Infinix devices come with pre-installed apps for social media, music, or utilities. Explore these apps to see if they offer customization options within their settings.

Advanced Options (if applicable):

- Developer Options (if available): For advanced users, some Infinix models might have a hidden "Developer Options" menu containing settings for animation speeds, background processes, and more. Proceed with caution as these options can potentially affect performance or stability if not used carefully.

13.1 Changing Themes and Wallpapers

Exploring Themes:

- Theme Stores: XOS often provides access to built-in theme stores or apps. These stores house a collection of themes that can drastically change the visual style of your phone's interface. They can include new wallpapers, icon packs, and even custom fonts (depending on the theme). Browse the available themes and download the one that suits your aesthetic preferences.
- Pre-installed Themes: Your Infinix device might come with a few pre-installed themes. Explore these themes to see if any resonate with you before diving into downloadable options.

Applying Themes:

- Theme App/Settings: Once you've found a theme you like, navigate to the theme app or theme settings (location might vary depending on your device model).
- Apply the Theme: Look for an "Apply" or "Use" button associated with the chosen theme. Selecting this button will typically change your phone's interface to the new theme.

Finding Wallpapers:

- Preloaded Wallpapers: Your Infinix device might come preloaded with a collection of wallpapers. You can access them through the wallpaper settings or gallery app.

- Downloading Wallpapers Online: Numerous websites and apps offer free and paid wallpapers. Explore these options to find an image that suits your style.

Setting Wallpapers:

- Wallpaper Settings: Navigate to the wallpaper settings on your Infinix Note 40 Pro/Pro+. This option might be within the display settings, personalization settings, or a dedicated wallpaper app (depending on your device model).
- Choose Your Wallpaper: Select the desired wallpaper image from your pre-loaded options, downloaded images, or from the gallery app.
- Set Wallpaper Position (if applicable): Some devices allow you to choose how the wallpaper is positioned on your home screen and lock screen (e.g., centered, tiled).

Additional Tips:

- Matching Themes & Wallpapers: Consider choosing a theme and wallpaper that complement each other visually for a more cohesive look.
- Live Wallpapers (if supported): Some Infinix models might support live wallpapers that add a dynamic element to your home screen. Explore this option if your device offers it.
- Customizing App Icons (if supported): A few Infinix models allow applying icon packs that change the appearance of app icons. This can further personalize the visual style of your device along with themes and wallpapers.

13.2 Customizing Ringtones and Notifications

Accessing Sound Settings:

1. Locate and tap on the Settings app on your home screen, usually represented by a gear or cog icon.
2. Navigate to the Sound & Vibration section within the Settings app. On some Infinix models, you might find it under Notifications or Ringtones.

Customizing Ringtones:

- Default Ringtone: In the Sound & Vibration settings, you will find an option for "Phone Ringtone" or "Default Ringtone." This allows you to set the ringtone that plays for incoming calls from contacts not assigned a specific ringtone.
- Ringtones for Specific Contacts: Many Infinix devices allow you to assign personalized ringtones to individual contacts. Find the "Contacts" option within the Sound & Vibration settings (or directly within the Contacts app on some models). Select a contact, then look for an option to "Set ringtone" or "Assign ringtone." Choose a desired ringtone from the pre-installed options on your device or from your downloaded audio files (if supported by your device model).

Managing Notification Sounds:

- App Notifications: Look for a section titled "App Notifications" or similar wording within the Sound & Vibration settings. This section will typically display a list of your installed apps.
- Individual App Settings: Tap on an app from the list to access its notification settings. You might see options to:
  - Enable or disable notifications for that specific app.
  - Choose a notification sound from pre-loaded options or your downloaded audio files (if supported).
  - Select a vibration pattern (on some models) to accompany the notification sound.

Additional Tips:

- Volume Control: Don't forget to adjust the ringer and notification volume levels using the volume buttons on the side of your phone. You can also find volume controls within the Sound & Vibration settings.
- Silent Mode: For situations where you don't want to be disturbed, you can enable Silent mode on your Infinix Note 40 Pro/Pro+. Silent mode typically silences ringtones and notifications, but you might be able to configure it to vibrate for calls while keeping notifications silent (options might vary).
- Do Not Disturb: Some Infinix models might offer a "Do Not Disturb" mode that allows you to schedule quiet times when calls and notifications are silenced. Explore your Do Not Disturb settings (if available) to customize it according to your needs.

13.3 Adjusting Launcher Settings

The launcher on your Infinix Note 40 Pro/Pro+ is the core of your home screen experience. It controls how your apps, widgets, and folders are arranged and accessed. XOS, the operating system on your device, offers various launcher settings to personalize your home screen for optimal usability and a touch of your style.

Accessing Launcher Settings:

The exact method to access launcher settings might differ slightly depending on your Infinix model. Here are two common ways:

- Long press on an empty space on the home screen: This usually opens a home screen customization menu where you might find a shortcut to launcher settings (e.g., "Home settings," "Launcher settings").
- Navigate through app settings: Open the Settings app and look for a section titled "Home screen," "Launcher," or similar wording.

Common Launcher Settings:

Once you've accessed your launcher settings, you'll likely find options to adjust various aspects of your home screen:

- Home Screen Layout: Change the number of home screens (swipe-able pages) and the grid size (number of rows and columns) for app icons.

- App Drawer Style: Modify the layout and style of your app drawer, where all your installed apps are listed.
- Dock Settings: Manage the app dock at the bottom of your home screen. You can add or remove apps from the dock for quick access.
- Wallpaper & Themes: While these settings might be in separate menus on some models, launcher settings might also provide options for changing your wallpaper and applying themes that can alter the overall look and feel of your home screen.
- Icon Gestures (if supported): Some launchers allow assigning custom actions to swiping up, down, or holding on app icons for quick access to specific app functions.
- Hide Apps: This option, if available, lets you hide apps from your app drawer without uninstalling them.
- Search Bar: Enable or disable the search bar on your home screen, used for searching installed apps and contacts.

Additional Tips:

- Explore All Options: Take some time to explore all the launcher settings available on your Infinix device. You might discover hidden gems that significantly enhance your home screen experience.
- Third-party Launchers: While XOS offers its launcher, you can also install third-party launcher apps from the Google Play Store to unlock even more customization options and features for your home screen.
- Default Launcher: If you install a third-party launcher and want to make it your default, you might find this option within the launcher settings or in the general device settings under "Apps" or "Default apps" (terminology might vary).

Chapter 14: Exploring Unique XOS Features

Visual Enhancements:

- Theme Store (possible): XOS often boasts a theme store packed with downloadable themes that can entirely transform the look and feel of your phone's interface, including wallpapers, icons, and accent colors. Explore the themes and find one that matches your style.
- Eye Care: This feature adjusts the screen colors to reduce blue light emission, potentially reducing eye strain during extended reading or use in low-light environments.

Performance and Optimization:

- XOS Security (or similar): This built-in app suite might offer functionalities like app permission management, system scans for malware, and battery optimization tools to keep your device secure and running smoothly.
- Dar-Link (or similar gaming features): Some Infinix models come with XOS features geared towards gamers. Dar-Link (or similar names) might intelligently allocate resources during gameplay to ensure smooth performance and reduce frame drops.

- Smart Freeze (or App Freezer): This feature (if available) lets you temporarily freeze unused apps, potentially freeing up system resources and extending battery life.

Multitasking and Convenience Features:

- Video Assistant (possible): This feature (if available) might offer tools for enhancing your video viewing experience, like subtitle adjustments or video playback controls in a floating window.
- Lightning Multi-Window: This feature allows you to run two apps simultaneously in resizable floating windows, enabling multitasking and quick switching between tasks.
- XClone (or App Cloner): This feature (if available) lets you create clones of your social media or messaging apps, essentially creating two separate accounts usable on the same phone.

Advanced Features (Explore with Caution):

- Developer Options (hidden menu): For advanced users, some Infinix models might have a hidden "Developer Options" menu containing settings for animation speeds, background processes, and more. Be cautious when exploring these settings, as they can potentially affect performance or stability if not used carefully.

Please remember: The specific XOS features available on your Infinix Note 40 Pro/Pro+ might vary depending on your device model and XOS version.

14.1 Using the Folax Voice Assistant

- Wake Word (if enabled): Some Infinix models allow setting up a wake word (like "Hi Folax" or a custom phrase) to activate the assistant with your voice. Look for a "Wake word" setting within the Folax settings or XOS settings to enable and choose your preferred phrase.
- App Button: Open the Folax app (if pre-installed) to launch the assistant and access its interface.
- Hardware Button (possible): A few Infinix devices might have a dedicated hardware button for activating Folax. Locate this button (usually on the side of the phone) and press it to start a voice interaction.

Using Voice Commands:

Once Folax is activated, speak your commands clearly. Here are some examples of what Folax can do:

- Basic Commands: Ask for the weather, current time, or perform basic math calculations.
- Make Calls & Send Messages: Use voice commands to initiate calls or send text messages to your contacts.
- Control Playback: Play, pause, or skip music and videos using voice commands.
- Open Apps: Ask Folax to launch specific applications on your phone.
- Set Alarms & Reminders: Instruct Folax to set alarms or create reminders for upcoming tasks.

- Search the Web: Ask Folax questions and perform web searches using your voice.

Folax's Capabilities (Explore Further):

The functionalities mentioned above are just a glimpse of what Folax can potentially do. Here's how to explore its full potential:

- Folax Settings: Dive deeper into the Folax app settings (if available) to discover more features and customize your voice assistant experience. You might find options for:
    - Changing the wake word (if supported)
    - Adjusting voice recognition sensitivity
    - Setting preferred languages
    - Exploring specific command categories (e.g., music control, device settings)
- Online Resources: Search online for Infinix user manuals or support pages specific to your device model. These resources might provide more detailed information on Folax's functionalities and supported voice commands.

Remember: Folax is still under development, and its performance might improve with future updates. Be patient with occasional limitations and keep an eye out for software updates that might enhance Folax's capabilities.

14.2 Enabling Lightning Multi-Window

Lightning Multi-Window, a valuable feature on your Infinix Note 40 Pro/Pro+ powered by XOS, allows you to run two apps simultaneously in resizable windows. This functionality enhances multitasking capabilities, letting you switch between tasks efficiently.

Activating Lightning Multi-Window (Method 1: Three-Finger Swipe):

1. Ensure the feature is enabled: Navigate to your Settings app and locate the XOS Features section (or similar wording depending on your model). Look for an option titled Lightning Multi-Window or Multi-Window. If it's disabled, toggle the switch to ON.
2. Three-Finger Swipe Up: Once enabled, swipe upwards on your screen using three fingers from the bottom bezel (the area below the screen). This gesture should trigger Lightning Multi-Window mode.
3. Selecting the Second App: You'll see a list of your recently used apps along the top or bottom portion of the screen (depending on your model). Choose the second app you want to run in the multi-window view.
4. Resizing and Positioning Windows: Each app will occupy half of the screen by default. You can drag the dividing line in the center to resize the windows according to your preference. You can also drag the top of a window to reposition it to the top or bottom of the screen.

Activating Lightning Multi-Window (Method 2: Recent Apps Button):

1. Enable Lightning Multi-Window (if not already done using Method 1).
2. Open the First App: Launch the first app you want to use in the multi-window view.
3. Recent Apps Button: Tap the Recent Apps button (usually the left virtual button on the navigation bar at the bottom of your screen). This will display your recently used applications.
4. App Icon Menu (Three Dots): Locate the first app you launched for multi-windowing. Tap the menu icon (usually three vertical dots) associated with the app icon in the recent apps list.
5. Select "Enter Split Screen" or Similar Option: The menu should display an option like "Enter Split Screen" or "Use in Split Screen." Tap this option to launch the selected app in a multi-window view.
6. Choosing the Second App: The same way you did in Method 1, select the second app you want to run alongside the first app in the multi-window view.
7. Resizing and Positioning Windows (as in Method 1): You can resize and reposition the windows using the dividing line and dragging motions as described in Method 1.

Exiting Lightning Multi-Window:

- Swipe down on the top bar of the app you want to close (the one that occupies the top portion of the screen by default). Alternatively, you can swipe upwards from the bottom bezel using one finger (instead of three fingers for activating).

- You can also tap the home button to exit multi-window mode and return to your home screen. The previously used apps will still be running in the background.

Additional Tips:

- Supported Apps: Ensure the apps you want to use in multi-window mode are compatible with Lightning Multi-Window. Most apps should work, but some might not be optimized for this feature.
- Navigation in Multi-Window: You can switch between the two multi-window apps by swiping left or right on the dividing line or by tapping on the app window you want to interact with.
- Fullscreen Mode: Tap and hold the dividing line to maximize one window and use it in fullscreen mode. Swipe down on the top bar of the maximized window to return it to its previous size in the multi-window view.

14.3 Creating Custom Gestures

While creating custom gestures for system-wide actions might not be a native feature on most Infinix devices with XOS, there are alternative methods you can explore to achieve similar functionality:

Launcher Customization (Limited):

- Icon Gestures (possible): Some Infinix launcher settings might offer the ability to assign custom actions to swiping up, down, or holding on app icons. This can be a shortcut to perform specific functions within an app without needing to launch it fully.

Third-Party Launcher Apps:

- Advanced Customization: Consider installing a third-party launcher app from the Google Play Store. Many launchers offer extensive customization options, including the ability to assign custom gestures (swipes, taps, holds) to launch apps, perform actions, or open shortcuts.

Accessibility Features (Potential Workaround):

- AssistiveTouch (similar features): Some Infinix models might have accessibility features like AssistiveTouch (terminology might vary). These features can create a floating button or menu overlay that provides shortcuts to various functions, including launching apps or simulating some gestures. While not exactly creating custom gestures, it can offer a similar benefit of quick access to specific actions.

Remember:

- Device Model Variations: These functionalities may vary depending on your specific Infinix model and XOS version. Consult your user manual or search online for your device model to find the most up-to-date information on launcher customization options or accessibility features.
- Third-Party Launcher Risks: Before installing a third-party launcher app, be cautious about app permissions and download only from reputable sources on the Google Play Store.

Glossary of Phone Lingo

Here's a glossary of common phone lingo terms you might encounter:

General Terms:

- Smartphone: A mobile phone with advanced capabilities like a web browser, email, and the ability to run apps.
- Feature Phone: A basic mobile phone with limited functionality compared to a smartphone, typically used for calling, texting, and basic multimedia.
- SIM Card (Subscriber Identity Module): A small chip containing your phone number and subscription information used to connect to a cellular network.
- OS (Operating System): The software that controls the core functionality of your phone, like Android or iOS.
- App (Application): A software program designed to run on a phone for various purposes like games, social media, or productivity tools.
- UI (User Interface): The way you interact with your phone, including the visual elements and layout on the screen.
- UX (User Experience): The overall experience of using your phone, encompassing ease of use, efficiency, and enjoyment.

Hardware Terms:

- Display: The screen of your phone where you see visuals and interact with the UI.
- Camera: The digital camera built into your phone for taking photos and videos.
- Battery: The power source that keeps your phone running.
- Processor: The central chip that processes information and performs calculations on your phone.
- RAM (Random Access Memory): Temporary memory that stores information currently being used by apps.
- Storage: The internal memory of your phone that stores apps, data, photos, and other files.

Network Terms:

- Cellular Network: A network of towers that allows your phone to connect to make calls, send texts, and use mobile data.
- Mobile Data: Data transmitted wirelessly over a cellular network to access the internet on your phone.
- Wi-Fi: A wireless networking technology that allows your phone to connect to the internet through a router.
- Bluetooth: A short-range wireless technology for connecting your phone to other devices like headphones or speakers.
- GPS (Global Positioning System): A satellite-based system that provides location information to your phone for maps and navigation apps.

Call & Messaging Terms:

- Call: A voice conversation between two or more people using their phones.
- Text Message (SMS): A short message sent between phones using text.
- MMS (Multimedia Messaging Service): A message that can include text, pictures, videos, and audio.
- Video Call: A call where you can see the person you're talking to on video.
- Voicemail: A voicemail service stores voice messages from callers when you can't answer your phone.

Smartphone Specific Terms:

- App Store: An online store where you can download and install apps on your phone (e.g., Google Play Store, Apple App Store).
- Notification: An alert on your phone that informs you about something, like a new message or email.
- Widget: A small, interactive app that displays information or allows you to perform quick actions directly on your home screen.
- Streaming: Watching or listening to media (like videos or music) live over the internet instead of downloading it first.
- Bloatware: Unwanted pre-installed apps that come with your phone.

This is not an exhaustive list, but it covers a wide range of common phone lingo terms.

Conclusion

In conclusion, the Infinix Note 40 Pro and Pro+ are truly remarkable devices that offer a wide range of features and capabilities to meet the needs of modern smartphone users. With their powerful processors, high-quality cameras, and stunning displays, these devices are perfect for both personal and professional use.

Whether you're looking to capture and share your life's moments, stay connected with friends and family, or stay productive on-the-go, the Infinix Note 40 Pro and Pro+ have got you covered. The devices' long-lasting batteries, fast charging capabilities, and expandable storage options make them ideal for users who demand more from their smartphones.

Moreover, the Infinix Note 40 Pro and Pro+ come with a range of innovative features, such as the XPen stylus, which allows for precise and intuitive input for all your creative and productivity needs. The devices' customizable user interface and AI-powered features also make for a seamless and personalized user experience.

The Infinix Note 40 Pro and Pro+ aren't just smartphones; they're potential companions on your journey of exploration, creation, and connection. Whether you're a budding photographer capturing fleeting moments, a mobile gamer conquering virtual worlds, or a multitasker juggling work and play, these devices offer the power and versatility to fuel your endeavors.

Overall, the Infinix Note 40 Pro and Pro+ are top-of-the-line devices that offer exceptional value for their price. With their sleek designs, advanced features, and reliable performance, these devices are sure to exceed your expectations and become an essential tool in your daily life.

So, unleash your creativity. Push the boundaries of what's possible. Capture breathtaking landscapes, dive into immersive games, or stay connected with loved ones near and far. The Infinix Note 40 Pro/Pro+ is more than just a device; it's a potential extension of yourself, waiting to be unlocked.

Thank you for taking the time to read this user guide, and we hope that it has been helpful in your exploration of the Infinix Note 40 Pro and Pro+. With this guide, you'll be able to make the most of your device's features and capabilities, and enjoy all that the Infinix Note 40 Pro and Pro+ have to offer.

Unveiling the Specs: A Deep Dive into the Infinix Note 40 Pro/Pro+ Technical Stuff

The Infinix Note 40 Pro and Pro+ pack a punch when it comes to technical specifications, offering features designed for performance and user experience. Here's a breakdown of the key specs to help you understand the technical capabilities of these devices:

Display:

- Size: Both the Note 40 Pro and Pro+ boast a large 6.78-inch display with FHD+ resolution (1080 x 2436 pixels). This translates to a crisp and vibrant viewing experience for multimedia content, gaming, and everyday tasks.
- Panel Technology (possible variations): Specs might differ slightly depending on your region, but the display could be either IPS LCD or AMOLED. IPS LCD panels offer good viewing angles and color reproduction, while AMOLED panels are known for deeper blacks, higher contrast, and potentially better battery efficiency.

Performance:

- Processor: Both devices come equipped with the MediaTek Dimensity 7020 processor. This octa-core chipset is designed for mid-range devices, offering a balance between performance and battery efficiency. It can handle everyday tasks, gaming, and multitasking with relative ease.

- RAM: Here's where the Pro and Pro+ models diverge. The Note 40 Pro offers 8GB of RAM, while the Pro+ bumps it up to 12GB. RAM allows apps to run smoothly and helps with multitasking. Having 12GB of RAM on the Pro+ can be beneficial for users who run demanding apps or games simultaneously.

Storage:

- Both models come with 256GB of storage, offering ample space for apps, photos, videos, and other files.

Cameras:

- Rear Camera System: Both devices sport a quad-camera rear system. The primary sensor is a powerful 108-megapixel lens, accompanied by likely secondary sensors for ultra-wide, macro, and depth information. This setup allows for capturing high-resolution photos with impressive detail, along with wide-angle shots and close-up focus options.
- Front Camera: Both models feature a 32-megapixel front-facing camera for capturing selfies and facilitating video calls.

Battery:

- Capacity: Here's another point of differentiation. The Note 40 Pro packs a 5000mAh battery, while the Pro+ boasts a slightly smaller 4600mAh battery. Both capacities are generous and should provide a full day's worth of use for most users, depending on usage patterns.

- Charging: The Note 40 Pro supports 20W fast charging, while the Pro+ takes things a step further with support for faster 100W charging technology. This allows the Pro+ to be charged significantly faster, ideal for users who need their phone powered up quickly.
- Wireless Charging (Pro+ only): An exciting feature exclusive to the Pro+ model is support for wireless charging. This eliminates the need for cables and allows you to charge your phone by placing it on a compatible wireless charging pad (sold separately).

Software:

- Operating System: Both devices run on Android 14, the latest iteration of the Android operating system at the time of the Infinix Note 40 Pro/Pro+ launch (April 2024). This ensures access to the latest features and security updates from Google.
- XOS Customization: On top of Android 14, Infinix devices run on their custom interface, XOS. XOS offers additional features, themes, and customizations compared to stock Android.

Additional Considerations:

- Build Quality: Infinix phones are generally known for their plastic construction. While some users prefer a premium metal or glass feel, plastic can keep the weight down and offer durability.
- Fingerprint Sensor: Both models likely incorporate an in-display fingerprint sensor for secure unlocking.

The Infinix Note 40 Pro and Pro+ offer compelling technical specifications targeted towards users who prioritize performance, powerful cameras, and long battery life. The Pro+ model takes things a step further with faster charging, wireless charging capabilities, and potentially an AMOLED display (depending on the specific model). Ultimately, the best choice between the Pro and Pro+ depends on your needs and budget. If you prioritize the fastest charging speeds, wireless charging, and the potential for a higher quality display, the Pro+ might be the way to go. If those features are less important and you prefer a slightly lower price point, the Note 40 Pro remains a capable option.

Taming the Troubles: Troubleshooting Guide for Common Issues

Even the most powerful smartphones can encounter occasional glitches. If you're facing issues with your Infinix Note 40 Pro/Pro+, don't fret! This guide offers solutions to some commonly encountered problems to get your device running smoothly again.

Basic Troubleshooting Tips:

- Restart Your Phone: A simple restart can often resolve temporary glitches. Press and hold the power button, then tap "Restart" on the power menu.
- Check for Software Updates: Outdated software can sometimes cause issues. Navigate to your Settings > System > Software Update (or similar wording) and download and install any available updates.
- Manage Apps: Force close any misbehaving apps or uninstall them if they continue to cause problems. Go to Settings > Apps & notifications (or Apps), select the problematic app, then tap "Force Stop" or "Uninstall".

Addressing Specific Issues:

- Wi-Fi Connectivity Issues:
  - Forget and reconnect to the Wi-Fi network: Go to Settings > Wi-Fi, tap and hold the problematic network name, then tap "Forget network". Now,

rescan for available networks and reconnect with your Wi-Fi password.
- Restart your Wi-Fi router or modem.
- Check for weak signal strength and move closer to the router if necessary.

- Bluetooth Connectivity Issues:
  - Forget and re-pair Bluetooth devices: Go to Settings > Bluetooth, tap the paired device you're having trouble with, and tap "Forget". Then, pair the device again following the usual Bluetooth pairing process.
  - Restart your Bluetooth by toggling Bluetooth off and on in the Settings menu.

- Poor Battery Life:
  - Identify battery drainers: Go to Settings > Battery and check which apps are consuming the most battery. Consider reducing background activity or uninstalling apps with excessive battery drain.
  - Adjust screen brightness: Lowering screen brightness can significantly improve battery life.
  - Disable unnecessary features like Bluetooth or GPS when not in use.
  - Utilize battery saver mode: Battery saver mode reduces background activity and limits power consumption to extend battery life.

- App Crashes or Freezes:
  - Force close the app (as mentioned in basic troubleshooting tips).
  - Update the app: Outdated apps can sometimes malfunction. Open the Google Play Store, tap on your profile icon, then tap "Manage apps & device" > "Manage" to see if any app updates are available.

- o Reinstall the app: If updating doesn't resolve the issue, try uninstalling and reinstalling the app.
- Performance Issues (Slowness, Lag):
  - o Restart your phone (as mentioned in basic troubleshooting tips).
  - o Close unnecessary background apps: Too many apps running simultaneously can slow down your phone.
  - o Check for storage space: If your phone's storage is nearing capacity, it can impact performance. Consider deleting unnecessary files or transferring them to an SD card (if your model supports expandable storage).

Advanced Troubleshooting:

- Factory Reset: If none of the above solutions work, a factory reset might be necessary. This erases all your data and settings, restoring your phone to its original state. Back up your data before performing a factory reset. The option can typically be found in Settings > System > Reset options (or similar wording).

Additional Resources:

- Infinix Support Website: The Infinix website might offer troubleshooting guides or FAQs specific to your device model. Search for your model number on the Infinix website for relevant support resources.
- Infinix User Forums: Online communities and forums dedicated to Infinix users can be a valuable resource for finding solutions to common problems and sharing experiences with other users.

Frequently Asked Questions (FAQ)

General

- What's the difference between the Infinix Note 40 Pro and Pro+?: The key differences lie in RAM, battery, charging, and potentially the display. The Pro+ boasts 12GB RAM compared to the Pro's 8GB, a slightly smaller 4600mAh battery (compared to the Pro's 5000mAh), but with support for much faster 100W charging (the Pro offers 20W). The Pro+ might also come with an AMOLED display, while the Pro might have an IPS LCD panel (depending on the region).
- What are the color options for the Infinix Note 40 Pro/Pro+?: Color options may vary depending on region, but common options might include Black, Silver, and Blue. Consult the official Infinix website or trusted retailers in your area for available color options.
- When will the Infinix Note 40 Pro/Pro+ be released?: The Infinix Note 40 Pro+ is expected to be released in April 2024 (information based on April 12, 2024). The release date for the Note 40 Pro might be slightly earlier. Always check with official sources or trusted retailers for confirmed release dates in your specific region.

Performance

- Is the Infinix Note 40 Pro/Pro+ good for gaming?: The MediaTek Dimensity 7020 processor is suitable for most games, but not necessarily top-of-the-line titles at the highest settings. The 8GB RAM on the Pro and 12GB RAM on the Pro+ will allow you to run multiple apps smoothly and enhance multitasking capabilities during gaming.

Camera

- How good is the camera on the Infinix Note 40 Pro/Pro+?: With a 108-megapixel main sensor and triple/quad rear camera system, the Note 40 Pro/Pro+ should capture high-resolution photos with good detail in most lighting conditions. The front-facing 32-megapixel camera is suitable for selfies and video calls.

Battery

- How long does the battery on the Infinix Note 40 Pro/Pro+ last?: Battery life depends on usage patterns. The 5000mAh battery on the Note 40 Pro and the 4600mAh battery on the Pro+ are both generous capacities and should provide a full day's worth of use for most users. The Pro+ boasts significantly faster 100W charging, allowing you to quickly top up the battery when needed.

Software

- What operating system does the Infinix Note 40 Pro/Pro+ run on?: Both devices run on Android 14, the latest version available at launch (April 2024). On top of Android, Infinix uses their XOS custom interface, offering additional features and customizations compared to stock Android.

www.ingramcontent.com/pod-product-compliance
Lightning Source LLC
Chambersburg PA
CBHW052206220526
45471CB00004B/1838